Caring Together
A Group Study Guide
for Anyone Involved in Caregiving

By Chris Morley

CARING TOGETHER
A Group Study Guide for Anyone Involved in Caregiving

Copyright © 2011 Chris Morley
Original edition published in English under the title
CARING TOGETHER by Kevin Mayhew Ltd, Buxhall, England.
This edition copyright © Fortress Press 2019

All rights reserved. Except for brief quotations in critical articles or reviews, no part of this book may be reproduced in any manner without prior written permission from the publisher. Email copyright@ augsburgfortress.org or write to Permissions, Fortress Press, PO Box 1209, Minneapolis, MN 55440-1209.

Scripture quotations are from The New Revised Standard Version of the Bible copyright 1989 by the Division of Christian Education of the National Council of Churches in the USA. Used by permission.
All Rights Reserved.

Cover image: Photo by Xesai on iStock
Cover design: Emily Wyland

Print ISBN: 978-1-5064-5911-0

Contents

Preface		5
Introduction		7
Session 1	The Task of Caregiving	17
Session 2	Looking after Yourself	25
Session 3	Failure	33
Session 4	Why Do I Care?	43
Session 5	Listening	51
Session 6	Trying to Understand	61
Session 7	Anger	69
Session 8	Getting Support	79
Session 9	Growing through Pain	89
Session 10	The Struggle and the Joy	99
Appendix 1	Confidentiality and Some Ground Rules for Discussions	107
Appendix 2	Notes on Structure	109
Bibliography		111

I'm very grateful to Janet Morley, Wendy Spray, and Barbara Tomkinson for their insights as this book developed and to my wife, Myriel, whose ideas and experience have influenced the book's content and whose patience and encouragement helped make it happen.

Preface

In thirty-eight years of ministry, I've seen some wonderful caregiving. Spouses who for decades have cared for partners with long-term illness or disability, parents who have given the most active years of their lives to look after their autistic child, people often themselves getting on in life committed to enabling their frail and elderly parents to get the most from their remaining years. I've seen people offer time-consuming, attentive support to neighbors who needed it, youth leaders showing extraordinary patience and perseverance in their mentoring of young people, pastoral caregivers in the church who loyally and thoughtfully have taken those they've been asked to care for under their wings. It's people like this to whom this study course is dedicated and who I hope will benefit from it.

I've also often admired the encouragement people involved in caring for others have offered each other. In practical ways, and in the even more important support given by just listening, those whose lives appear to be full already with care for others so often find the energy to offer more to fellow caregivers. Such mutual support is immensely valuable and I hope this book will encourage it. Some of those purchasing it will be part of a church community out of which a group to use its material could easily be formed. Most congregations would be surprised to find how many of their members are involved in caregiving in one way or another. Others may need to be more proactive in finding or forming a group in which the ideas in this book could be discussed. Many local authorities have a Caregivers Support Service who might well provide contact with other potential members of a group using this material.

Much of what this book contains I have taken from the experience of those years of offering support to people engaged in many different types of caregiving. More recently, I retired from full-time ministry myself a year or two early to care for my wife. Her spinal problems and rheumatoid arthritis restrict her mobility and cause increasing and constant pain. I began to learn about the challenge of this more focused kind of caregiving and realized how valuable a course such as this might be.

There's a strain of Christianity that encourages self-sacrifice for its own sake. We *ought* to be giving ourselves until it hurts; if we're not, we're somehow falling short. Many people have instilled in them, sometimes too deeply to be aware of it, a feeling that they're only worth anything if their lives are given to others. That's not what the gospel says. The message of Jesus was that each of us is intrinsically valuable without us having to *do* anything at all. What he offered was the freedom to be found in knowing that you are loved just as you are. I hope that's what those who use this book will rediscover. Through the mutual support the group offers and in the conversations the material in it encourages, people will, I hope, find their self-esteem boosted, their ability to enjoy life enhanced and therefore the quality of their caregiving deepened.

Introduction

This book will be most fruitfully used by a group. You may have purchased it because you're in a group that decides to use it or which was created for that purpose. You may, though, just have bought it because its topic appealed but, having looked at it, would like a group with whom to discuss it. If you are part of a church community, the church leaders might help in the setting up of such a group. If you aren't, the website associated with this book, www.caring-together.com, will have a list of where some current groups are meeting. (N.B. If you decide to start a group, please go to that website to let others know about it.)

Using this book

A group using this book could be open to anyone who regards themselves as a caregiver. Nearly everybody cares for somebody else at some time in their lives. When someone we know needs support, either during a temporary illness or in the longer term, we often rally around and do what we can to help. We might be called upon, sometimes for a comparatively short period, to take care of a relative, friend, neighbor, or fellow church member who is going through a time of illness or recovery. It might be elderly parents who need support or maybe we have a more general responsibility, perhaps for pastoral care within a church or professionally. This study book offers churches material that can be part of the pastoral support provided by the congregation to those in any of these kinds of situations.

The term "caregiver" also has a more technical meaning. The word describes someone of any age who provides unpaid support to family or friends who could not manage without this help. This could be caring for a relative, partner, or friend who is ill, frail, disabled, or has mental health or substance abuse problems.

There are about six million such people in the UK, about one in ten of the population, and they are from all walks of life, all cultures, and can be of any age. Caregivers in this, as well as in the more general, sense will find working through this book within a supportive group highly beneficial.

The topic is approached from the standpoint of faith, as evidenced by the biblical study that lies at the heart of each session and the important suggestions about praying for each other. But the challenge of being a caregiver is not unique to committed Christians and the incorporation of material from secular as well as religious sources makes this suitable material for any group of caregivers.

People receiving care are very different from each other. Some may be virtually incapable of communication or too ill to be bothered with it, while others may relish a long conversation to relieve the boredom. So parts of the material will not be equally applicable to every situation and can be adapted to suit. Similarly the circumstances of each person doing the caregiving are different. For some, especially full-time caregivers, a sudden emergency or sheer exhaustion may make attendance at one or more of the sessions impossible. This is perfectly appropriate and group members will no doubt both understand this and keep the absentee in touch. Some may find coming to the group difficult because there's no one to be with the one they're caring for while they're attending it. It would be good if the host church could help here, either with a volunteer or with financial support so that agency cover can be arranged.

How is the book organized?

There are ten sessions that can be held with a regularity that suits each individual group. It's best if every member of the group can attend every meeting so their frequency should be realistic. Each group member will need a copy of the book. Sessions need to be long enough to allow good discussion and so I recommend about two hours (see below). The sessions are designed for small groups of four to six people. Groups that are larger than this may well find that the discussions take longer. In that case you could divide into smaller groups for some of the discussion sessions or extend the length of the series of meetings and spread the material for each session over more than one meeting. Appendix 2 gives some guidance about this.

The role of the group leader

The leader's task is to enable the group members to gain as much as possible from the group and to contribute to it as much as they want to. There are many things this will involve.

Find a suitable location—a comfortable room in a church or in someone's home. It's not appropriate for the group to meet in the home of a member of the group—someone in their own home would find it harder to unwind and take full advantage of the sessions. The space should be big enough so that everyone can see everyone else in the group—eye contact and body language often communicate as much as words.

Liaise with the sponsoring church, if a church is running the course. Members of the local congregation may among other things:

- help with refreshments if the meetings are at the church.
- provide a volunteer who can look after someone being cared for so that their caregiver may attend the group.
- pray for the group.

If required, download for each session the opening song and the recording of the author reading his comments on the Bible passage. These are available on www.caring-together.com.

They may be played to the group from the hard drive of a computer or from a CD.

Make sure everyone in the group has been able to contribute to decisions about the timing and structure of the group. The leader needs to ensure everyone understands and accepts the agreements about confidentiality and to check every so often that everyone's happy about them.

Guide the group through the material, which will require the leader to read through the chapter before the session. During the group this involves:

- leading the prayers or inviting someone else to do so; choosing readers to read the passages from books about caregiving and from the Bible that are quoted and inviting others to take the leading role in the material for the prayers at the end of each session. It would be good to give as many people as wish to a chance to lead in these ways.

- bringing the group back to the point whenever a digression is becoming unhelpful.

- making sure everyone who wishes to say something gets the chance to do so.

- moving on to the next question, or section, when appropriate. A balance needs to be struck between the need to continue valuable conversation to an appropriate finishing point and the requirements of the overall balance of the session. The group will feel more secure if they know time boundaries are being maintained.

The leader will also need to let anyone who misses a session know about future arrangements. If preferred, the role can be divided, with one person leading the sessions and another fulfilling the more administrative, organizational tasks.

Who should lead the group?

One option is to choose a leader from within the church or organizing group. It is best if the leader is not someone who is currently a caregiver or who has a particularly demanding relationship they wish to focus on. But the leader should be someone who is sensitive to the needs of caregivers, perhaps someone with extensive pastoral experience or someone who has been but is no longer involved in a caregiving relationship. They also need to be able to use the set questions to guide a conversation without allowing them to dominate the way the discussion develops. Group members should be free to raise their own issues but within the boundaries set by the material for the session. The leader needs to be supportive and not judgmental, accepting not critical, firm but not domineering, and a good listener.

Another option would be to invite someone who has particular expertise to offer. There may of course be someone from within the church in this category but, if not, a little research could produce someone from the local community or from a nearby church—a therapist or counselor who works with groups, or someone from the local social services or voluntary sector who's experienced in working with small groups.

The leader may well benefit from knowing there is someone they can go to for advice or support. The material in this course could arouse strong feelings in the members of the group. Some of these will be expressed, others won't be. The leader might value the chance to talk over how the group is going with a third party, perhaps the minister or someone with the skills described in the previous paragraph. If this is going to happen, it needs to be spelled out in the first session's discussion about confidentiality.

Ground rules and confidentiality

It will be important to establish at the beginning some ground rules about how discussion should be conducted and what levels of confidentiality should be maintained. The group should refer to Appendix 1 for some ideas about confidentiality and for possible ground rules.

Flexibility

There may be times during the course when a major crisis occurs in the life of one of the members. If, for example, one of those being cared for by a group member dies or suffers a serious deterioration or accident, this will affect not just their caregiver but every member of the group. In such a situation, the group would probably need to break from using the material published here to allow time for mutual support or to adapt sessions accordingly.

The elements of each session

Here is a basic breakdown of what each session includes.

Opening reflection

A song is suggested, downloadable from www.kevinmayhew.com/caring-together-download.html
or from www.caring-together.com. The group can reflect on the words before praying together.

Gathering

Each person is invited to give their name and other information, which varies from session to session. After the first couple of sessions, giving your name will cease to be necessary as pure information. Some of the group will have come from a busy or stressful day—saying your name firmly and strongly is a way of saying to yourself and the group: whatever I have been doing today, now I am here! The other information (e.g. a hobby you have or something good that's happened this week) is included as a way of asserting the existence of life outside caregiving.

Exploring

This section provides an extended quotation about the experience of being a caregiver or being cared for. A member of the group should read the passage aloud and the group then discusses it together. There are questions provided but these are not prescriptive as other topics may emerge. The leader should be sensitive to what the group seems to want to discuss. There's absolutely no requirement to "get through" all the questions.

Reflecting

Next there is a reflection on a Bible passage. Someone should read the passage aloud and then the group can work through the author's comments. You can listen to these read by the author at www.caring-together.com or someone in the group can read them aloud. Again there are some suggested questions following this, intended to encourage conversation.

Learning

In all but the first session (in which time needs to be given to discussing confidentiality and ground rules), there is information about an insight into caregiving from a particular theological or psychological point of view. This is followed by a shorter period of discussion.

Preparation for the next session

It might be helpful and interesting for members of the group to explore in advance the insight into caregiving that will be introduced in the learning section of the next session and details of that are given at this point in the session. Information and links to relevant websites are available on the website www.caring-together.com. Some group members may not have internet access; perhaps those who have could pair off with people who haven't so the resource can be shared.

Prayers

There are suggestions for prayer as the session draws to an end. They offer a clear structure that will make it easier for those who may not be used to praying. Some groups will be very comfortable with times of open prayer to which group members freely contribute. If this is preferred, the suggested material can be scrapped or become only part of the time set aside for prayer.

I've included in this a time in which group members can pray for those they care for. Going around the group in the order in which they are seated in the circle, each person mentions a name and this is followed by silence for everyone to pray for that person. Going around the circle prevents the insecurity of not knowing who is next to speak and it is assumed that everyone will want to offer a name. The silence should be long enough for the person mentioned to be concentrated on by the group before the next person speaks.

To take away

The session ends with a brief quotation or poem that summarizes the theme of the session. It isn't intended that this be read aloud or necessarily referred to in the group, just noticed by the participants as they come to the end of the session.

Suggested time frame for the sessions

Opening reflection	5 minutes
Gathering	10 minutes
	(20 in the first session)

Exploring	35 minutes
Reflecting	35 minutes
Learning	20 minutes
	(10 in the first session)
Preparation for the next session	5 minutes
Prayers	10 minutes

These timings assume a two-hour session. If less time is available, one possibility would be to divide into smaller groups for some of the discussion sessions. Another would be to extend the length of the series of meetings and to spread the material for each session over more than one meeting. Recommendations about how this might be done are in Appendix 2.

N.B. These timings are only for guidance. The group will discover how long it needs for the various parts of the program. Group members will feel more secure if they have some sense that time boundaries are being observed but freedom to allow important conversations to reach their natural close is vital.

Session 1
The Task of Caregiving

In this first session, we will discover something about the situations each of us is in, some of the basic issues involved in caregiving, and what this group might offer.

Opening reflection
Listen to "Bridge over troubled water" (available to download from www.kevinmayhew.com/caring-together-download.html or from www.caring-together.com).

A prayer to say together
**Caring God,
you've given us people to care for
and we need your support and each other's to do it well.
Be with us in these times together
that they might give us new strength and wisdom.
Grant that our caregiving may echo yours.
In the name of your Son, Jesus.
Amen.**

Confidentiality
Discuss the issues around confidentiality and agree on appropriate boundaries (see Appendix 1 for suggestions on this and ground rules).

Gathering
Each person introduces themselves with their name and why they've joined the group. They also tell the group some basic

information about the person they care for. (While some will have joined the group because they want to reflect generally on the caregiving they offer, it would still be helpful for them to focus on one person they care for. This is partly because that's the assumption lying behind the way the material in this book is presented. Also, more can be learned by concentrating on the particular rather than on generalities. If a member of the group has not had time to give thought to who they'd like to make the focus of their reflection during this course, they could tell the group about them at the next meeting.)

Exploring

Someone reads the following poem aloud

"Being there"
In the deepest depths of pain
of tiredness
of vulnerability

I need you.

I do not need your words
or wise advice.

I just need you.

You and me together
in the stillness.
Holding my hand as I weep,
cradling me in the warmth of your love.

In the silence,
together.
Easing the loneliness,
sharing the pain.

Just being beside me
in your unknowingness.
Knowing that you cannot know the detail
of my tortured mind,
can never plumb these depths of pain.

The comfort of your presence
brings healing.

Your hand on mine.
Your thoughts
so closely intertwined with mine
in a deep embrace
of love,
a deep acknowledgement of my needs . . .

that I need you
just
to be there.

Pat Marsh, Christian poet and retreat leader

Some possibilities for discussion
- Is there anything in this poem that rings a bell for you?
- "I need you" says the poet. How does it feel to be needed?
- The person who is the subject of the poem faces pain, tiredness, vulnerability, and loneliness. What are the main challenges facing someone being cared for?
- How do you feel about your "unkowingness," the fact that you can't know all the details or plumb the depths of the struggle of the person you care for?

Reflecting
Serving and being served:
Someone reads from John 13:3-5, 12-15

Jesus, knowing that the Father had given all things into his hands, and that he had come from God and was going to God, got up from the table, took off his outer robe, and tied a towel around himself. Then he poured water into a basin and began to wash the disciples' feet and to wipe them with the towel that was tied around him . . .

After he had washed their feet, had put on his robe and had returned to the table, he said to them, "Do you know what I have done to you? You call me Teacher and Lord, and you are right, for that is what I am. So if I, your Lord and Teacher, have washed your feet, you also ought to wash one another's feet. For I have set you an example that you also should do as I have done to you."

Comments

(If you would like to hear the author reading these himself please refer to www.caring-together.com)

Most of you, if not all, will be here because you are foot-washers, perhaps literally but certainly metaphorically. You give time and energy to meeting those needs that someone you care about can't meet for themselves. I'm in a similar position. My wife's spinal condition and her rheumatoid arthritis combine to cause her constant pain and to be unable to do many of the things I take for granted. It was as I reflected on the effect of this on our relationship and on me as her caregiver that the idea came of offering material for a group like this. The task of caregiving can be so demanding, particularly when it's part of a life that's busy in other ways too, that we never step back and reflect on what we can learn from the situation. But doing so can bring us a new self-awareness that can make us more effective in our caregiving.

In the discussion you've just had, you may have been thinking together about what it feels like to be needed. Certainly it gives us a lot of power over the person who needs us. In the incident we've just read about, Jesus recognizes his power and where it comes from—he'd come from God and was going back to him—and chooses to use it, not at all for his own advantage but for others'. So here he does what was often the job of a servant and washes the disciples' travel-worn feet. As in so much else that he does, we see in this action of Jesus an expression of God's character. That's how God uses his power, not for himself but for us.

I think the power we have over those we care for has the same source. It's God who gives us the lives we have, our personalities, and our potential for loving. And we choose to use that power as he did by becoming servants. Our lives and our gifts are a treasure God has placed into our hands—we want to use them gently and purposefully for the benefit of others. And in so doing, we are expressing something of God's character as well as our own.

But I think this phrase Jesus uses about coming from God and going back to him doesn't only tell us that Jesus was empowered by God; it also points to mutual love and care, to a profound intimacy between Jesus and his Father. In his giving of himself to others, Jesus knew the security and encouragement of knowing he was being held in God's constant care and strength. We too are offered that same promise that God will hold and support us in our serving of others. His intimate knowledge of us means that he knows just what support we need. He enters the deepest recesses of our lives, shares our deepest secrets, and does so with gentleness, courtesy, understanding, and respect. Particularly when life feels difficult, that can be very encouraging.

Our caregiving too can often take us into a close intimacy with those we're caring for. Indeed to care properly in the kind of situations we're in can sometimes feel as though we are invading their privacy in a way that feels uncomfortable. When Jesus says to the disciples, "I have set you an example," he's encouraging us to do our caregiving his way. This includes sharing other people's privacy with the same respect and gentleness he showed his disciples when he washed their feet and that he shows us.

One final point from this passage. "You ought to wash one another's feet," Jesus says. This is not just about serving; it's also about being served. It's a reciprocal caregiving. Most of us will feel that that is true of the caregiving we offer. What we get back from those we care for is different in kind from what we offer them but, if we are fortunate, it has a value all of its own. We treasure it and this group is partly a chance to celebrate that.

But the group is also a chance to "wash each other's feet"; to be here for each other, to learn from each other, and to discover the joy of letting ourselves receive as well as give. Allegedly, one of the besetting sins of caregivers is that they are poor at taking help for themselves. They feel more comfortable in a giving than a receiving role. You'll no doubt discover as you talk the truth or otherwise of that stereotype! But you wouldn't be here if you didn't feel these meetings could be helpful to you and it's important not to be afraid to ask if there are specific ways in which you feel you could be supported by the group. That's the kind of washing each other's feet Jesus recommended to his disciples. Done with gentleness and respect for privacy, such support can be a practical experience of God's all-embracing care for each of us.

Some possibilities for discussion
- Caregivers usually have the power to affect considerably the quality of life of the one they care for. How do you feel about having that power?
- In conversations in this group, you will want to respect the intimacy of your relationship with the person you're caring

for. Do you think this, or your loyalty to them, will make it hard for you to share honestly even within the confidentiality of this group how you are feeling about your caregiving?
- Jesus encouraged his disciples to care for each other. Is there any particular kind of support you'd like from this group?

Preparing for the next session

In the next session, we shall be talking about Pelagius and his conflict with Augustine of Hippo. You could prepare by googling these two people or by following the links on www.caring-together.com.

Prayers

Leader   Jesus said: "Come to me, all you that are weary and are carrying heavy burdens and I will give you rest." *(Matthew 11:28)*

Now is the time for anyone in the group to mention anything going on in their lives that they are finding difficult. When there has been time for everyone who wishes to speak, a silence follows, during which each quietly prays for the members of the group who have just spoken. Anyone who wishes to say a prayer out loud can also do so.

>Generous God,
>As we pray for each other, you meet us in our need.
>Grant us the resources we need for our caregiving
>and surround us with your love.
>**Amen.**
>
>God says: "Do not fear, I have called you by name, you are mine. When you pass through the waters, I will be with you . . . when you walk through fire you shall not be burned." *(Isaiah 43:1b-2)*

Now go around the group in turn and each person mention the name of someone they are caring for. Follow each mention by a long enough silence for that person to be prayed for silently by the group before the next persons speaks. Then all pray together:

>**Loving God,
>you promise to sustain all whose lives are hard.
>Grant those for whom we care
>your strength and your peace.
>Amen.**
>
>**May God bless us all till we meet again.
>Amen.**

To take away

Well, now that we have seen each other, if you believe in me, I'll believe in you. Is that a bargain?
>*The Unicorn in* Through the Looking Glass, *Lewis Carroll*

Session 2
Looking after Yourself

In this session, we will look at how to balance caring for another with caring for ourselves.

Opening reflection
Listen to "One day at a time, sweet Jesus" (available to download from www.kevinmayhew.com/caring-together-download.html or from www.caring-together.com).

A prayer to say together
Generous God,
Jesus experienced directly
how fragile and frail human beings are.
But he also showed us what we can become.
Help us find ways to develop our potential,
to enhance our capacity to receive as well as give,
to find delight as well as challenge in life.
And, sweet Jesus, give us the strength to do this today.
In the name of your Son, Jesus.
Amen.

Gathering
Each person should take about a minute to give their name and to describe one of their strategies for coping and how it helps.

Then take time to review the experience of the first session and decide on any changes the group may want to make to the structure of the meeting.

Exploring

Sheila Cassidy ran a hospice caring for the dying.

More than anything I have learned that we are all frail people, vulnerable and wounded: it is just that some of us are more clever at concealing it than others! And of course the great joke is that it is OK to be frail and wounded because that is the way the Almighty transcendent God made people. The world is not divided into the strong who care and the weak who are cared for. We must each in turn care and be cared for, not just because it is good for us, but because that is the way things are. The hardest thing for those of us who are professional caregivers is to admit that we are in need, peel off our sweaty socks, and let someone else wash our dirty blistered feet. And when at last we have given in and have allowed someone to care for us, perhaps there is a certain inertia which makes us want to cling to the role of patient, reluctant to take up the task of serving once more. It is easy to forget that so much caregiving, so much serving is done by people who are weary and in some way not quite whole. Because we want our caregivers to be strong and invulnerable, we project onto them qualities which in fact they do not have. But again, perhaps that is the way things are because that is the way people are, and we must learn to be strong for those who need us most urgently and relax and lower our guard with those who are able to accept our weakness and to cherish us.

Some possibilities for discussion
- Is there anything in this account that rings a bell for you?
- Is Sheila Cassidy right that we tend to hide our vulnerability? If so, why?
- Is the person you care for able to care for you? If so, in what ways do they do that?

- Does the person you care for expect you to be "strong and invulnerable"? Are there times, as Sheila Cassidy suggests, when you need to pretend to a strength that isn't actually there?

Reflecting

Loving begins with yourself:

Someone reads from Mark 12:28-34

> One of the scribes came near and heard them disputing with one another, and seeing that [Jesus] answered them well, he asked him, "Which commandment is the first of all?" Jesus answered, "The first is: 'Hear, O Israel: the Lord our God, the Lord is one; you shall love the Lord your God with all your heart, and with all your soul, and with all your mind, and with all your strength.' The second is this, 'You shall love your neighbour as yourself.' There is no other commandment greater than these." Then the scribe said to him, "You are right, Teacher; you have truly said that 'he is one and beside him there is no other'; and 'to love him with all the heart, with all the understanding, and with all the strength,' and 'to love one's neighbour as oneself,'—this is much more important than all whole burnt offerings and sacrifices." When Jesus saw that he answered wisely, he said to him, "You are not far from the kingdom of God." After that no one dared ask him any question.

Comments

(If you would like to hear the author reading these himself please refer to www.caring-together.com)

The way some words sound backs up their meaning. For me the word "weary" is such a one. Its sound communicates that sense of heaviness and effort that is part of profound tiredness.

"Drained" is another one—it somehow suggests a delving into the depths to draw out the final dregs of energy and then finding nothing there. Of course there are many different kinds of tiredness—physical exhaustion doesn't infiltrate our whole being as emotional weariness does and it tends to make sleep easier rather than harder. Pressure and stress on the other hand tend not only to tire us in a way that affects our souls as well as our bodies but to keep us awake and so deny us nature's recuperation. That's the kind of tiredness that is not only not good for us, it makes our care much less effective.

Ogden Nash in his poem, *Prayer at the End of a Rope,* describes well this kind of stress:

> One little moment thy servant craves
> of being his own master.
> One placid vale beneath the waves
> of duty and disaster.
>
> Let me not bite more off the cob
> than I have teeth to chew;
> please let me finish just one job
> before the next is due.

Nash, in his characteristically humorous way, has put his finger on one of the prime causes of this kind of pressure—the feeling of constantly having to react to events rather than being in control of them. Sometimes of course we do have to respond to crises but there are also times when because we are already too tired to take charge of events, they threaten to overwhelm us. What we need to do of course is to spot the moment *before* it all gets too much and do something about our tiredness—once we're on the downward slope, it's very hard to stop.

But what can we do? How can we take time to look after ourselves if life's demands and the needs of the person we're caring for seem to consume every minute of the day? One technique is to practise stopping, or rather to use times when we're forced to stop, creatively. There are many moments in the course of even the busiest day when there's a natural pause—a traffic jam, waiting for the microwave or the bus, even going to the bathroom—and these can be used to take a breath, consciously calm ourselves, make contact with our deeper selves and with the source of our energy. This is one way of giving ourselves that little moment that we, like Ogden Nash, crave of being our own master.

We also need longer times of stopping, time that is genuinely ours to do with as we wish and time when we are not too weary to use it creatively. You can help each other in the discussion in a moment by talking about how each of you ensures you have sufficient time for yourselves. Doing so will improve our caregiving. Because when Jesus says we should love our neighbors as ourselves, he's recognizing that if we don't look after ourselves, we won't be able effectively to care for others.

But why wouldn't we look after ourselves? Most of us were taught to believe that human nature is basically selfish and that we should always be on our guard against giving in to that selfishness. This is what drives us into overdoing it. We are so determined not to put ourselves first that we go on giving to others to the point where it's bad for us and undermines the effectiveness of our caregiving. Such a notion damages us—it's a major cause of overwork and of pushing ourselves too hard. That's why Jesus was so wise to say we need to love others as ourselves. The assumption many of us have inherited that it's good to be self-sacrificial needs to be balanced by the need for self-care. We should put the same detailed, practical thoughtfulness into working out how best to look after ourselves as we do into caring for others.

But first we need somehow to be convinced that to love ourselves in that way is OK. That belief comes from faith. The central element of the Christian gospel is the belief that God loves each one of us regardless of our behavior. Good, bad, lazy, energetic, compassionate, selfish, whatever kind of person we are, God loves us. That's the truth the Bible says sets us free, and it does, it liberates us from any sense that to really look after our own needs, as well as others', is somehow wrong. If God loves us without us having to do anything to deserve it, that's how we should love ourselves.

So, though an important part of caring for ourselves involves the practicalities of making space for ourselves, an even more fundamental need is to make time for God, time when we can be reminded of God's unconditional love for us, time just to let God love us as we are and to be conscious that God is doing so. That habit can lead to the creation of all sorts of other valuable ones because it'll set us free to really take our own need to be cared for seriously.

Some possibilities for discussion
- Do you find it difficult to ask for what you need or take time for yourself? If so, why?
- Share ideas about how much time each of us needs "for ourselves" and how best to organize that.
- The comments suggest we need the nourishment that comes from spending time with God. Where do we find spiritual nourishment?

Learning

The fourth-century monk Pelagius believed that a newborn child was essentially good and reflected the image of God. Evil could imprison and disable that essential self but with God's help it could be liberated. His contemporary, St Augustine of Hippo, on the other hand, asserted that a baby was innately tainted by the sin of Adam, that he or she inherited Adam's "original sin." The image of God in a child needed to be restored in the sacrament of baptism. Augustine's view became orthodox partly because it was thought that Pelagius played down the need for Christ's help in reflecting his image in our later lives.

Perhaps humans do feel innately unworthy and this was the truth that Augustine latched onto. But, for whatever reason, down the ages Christianity's view of human nature as deficient has been more influential than the gospel's claim that God loves and treasures each of us. As was mentioned in the "Comments" section, many people more readily see themselves as unworthy and undeserving than regard themselves as to be treasured and cared for. One way people try to become worthy and deserving is by pushing themselves to achieve, sometimes with considerable self-sacrifice.

Some possibilities for discussion
- Share your individual reactions to these theories.
- How do you see yourself—essentially good and lovable as Pelagius did, or tainted and undeserving of love as Augustine did? Does this affect your willingness to care for yourself?
- Is there any level at which you feel you must keep going because your self-respect and/or God's love for you depend on it?

Preparing for the next session

At the start of the next session, each person will be sharing a photo they want to show the group. You'll need to remember to bring yours with you! It may be of the person(s) you care for or of something quite different.

In the next session, we shall be talking about Cognitive Behavioral Therapy. More information can be found by following the links on www.caring-together.com.

Prayers

Leader Even though I walk through the darkest valley, I fear no evil; for you, Lord, are with me. *(Psalm 23:4)*

Now is the time for anyone in the group to mention anything going on in their lives that they are finding difficult. When there has been time for everyone who wishes to speak, a silence follows, during which each quietly prays for the members of the group who have just spoken. Anyone who wishes to say a prayer out loud can also do so.

> Generous God,
> as we pray for each other, you meet us in our need.
> Grant us the resources we need for our caregiving
> and surround us with your love.
> **Amen.**

> Jesus said: "Do not let your hearts be troubled. Believe in God, believe also in me." *(John 14:1)*

Now go around the group in turn and each person mention the name of someone they are caring for. Follow each mention by a long enough silence for that person to be prayed for silently by the group before the next person speaks. Then all pray together:

> **Loving God,
> you promise to sustain all whose lives are hard.
> Grant those for whom we care
> your strength and your peace.
> Amen.**

> **May God bless us all till we meet again.
> Amen.**

To take away

Only what is really oneself has the power to heal.

Carl Gustav Jung

Session 3
Failure

In this session, we will explore the sense of inadequacy caregivers often feel and look at how to deal with feelings of failure.

Opening reflection
Listen to "Yesterday" (available to download from www.kevinmayhew.com/caring-together-download.html or from www.caring-together.com).

A prayer to say together
Generous God,
you see our failures more clearly than we do
and are more generous in forgiving them than we are.
Often our blaming of ourselves hangs over us like a shadow.
We wish we could undo any harm we've done.
Take away from us any longing to hide away
that we may stand boldly before you
conscious of your understanding and continuing love.
Help us to learn from what happened yesterday
that tomorrow we may be more wise and loving.
Through Jesus Christ our Lord.
Amen.

Gathering
Each person takes about a minute to remind the group of their name and to show a photograph if they've brought one or, if they haven't, to describe the photo they would have brought if they had remembered!

Exploring

When Marianne Talbot's mother began to suffer from Alzheimer's disease Marianne started writing blogs about the experience. Here she writes about her feelings of guilt.

Jan 28th 2009

In mum's (residential) home there's a book for recording arrivals and departures. I am sometimes shocked to see it's two or three days since I visited mum. You might ask why this should bother me: mum neither knows nor cares whether I visit. She can be sublimely indifferent to my presence, or even make it clear that she'd rather I wasn't there. So why should I feel guilty for missing a few days?

Interesting question that. In fact the whole question of guilt and caring is interesting. Because of my proximity, I am the only person to visit mum regularly. How come the one that does most visiting feels the most guilt?

But I feel less guilt now than I did when mum lived with me. Then I felt constantly guilty. Probably because I was constantly aware of everything I wasn't doing. Why, though, couldn't I have banished the guilt by reminding myself of what I was doing? Again why should the one who does the most also feel the most guilt?

This guilt haunts nearly every carer. As a carer you never feel you are doing enough. And however serene you appear you cannot but be guiltily aware of the ever-present fear you might explode. It comes back to responsibility. If you are a carer, then unless you are able to convince yourself you are doing everything you can, you will feel guilt. But who can take responsibility for the health and happiness of another human being, and really convince themselves they're doing everything they can?

... It seems to me that the guilt that is so much a part

of being a carer comes back to love. If you love someone who becomes unable to care for themselves then you will feel responsible for them, whether or not you formally take on responsibility for them. Guilt comes with that sense of responsibility.

Tough, isn't it? But when you're next overwhelmed with guilt, try congratulating yourself on your capacity for love, and remember what you are doing, instead of beating yourself up for everything else.

Keeping Mum, *Marianne Talbot*

Some possibilities for discussion
- Is there anything in this account that rings a bell for you?
- Marianne Talbot felt less guilty when her mother was in a home. Discuss the issues surrounding continuing to care for someone at home as well as those around finding residential care for them.
- Discuss aspects of caregiving that relate particularly in situations where the person being cared for isn't able to be aware of it.
- Marianne Talbot feels that her unexpressed feelings are so strong she might one day explode. Do you have any sense of guilt about how you feel in relation to the caregiving you offer? Are there any feelings you keep inside you because you'd feel guilty if you let them out? Or any you bottle up for fear of what might happen if you expressed them?

Reflecting

Simon Peter failed Jesus during the period just before his crucifixion by three times denying that he knew him. In this incident, after the resurrection, Jesus three times challenges Peter. Dealing with failure:

Someone reads from John 21:15-17

> When they had finished breakfast, Jesus said to Simon Peter, "Simon son of John, do you love me more than these?" He said to him, "Yes, Lord; you know that I love you." Jesus said to him, "Feed my lambs." A second time he said to him, "Simon son of John, do you love me?" He said to him, "Yes, Lord; you know that I love you." Jesus said to him, "Tend my sheep." He said to him the third time, "Simon son of John, do you love me?" Peter felt hurt because he said to him the third time, "Do you love me?" And he said to him, "Lord, you know everything; you know that I love you." Jesus said to him, "Feed my sheep."

Comments

(If you would like to hear the author reading these himself please refer to www.caring-together.com)

The conversation between Peter and Jesus described in the reading seems to be directly related to Peter's denial of Jesus. Lurking in the shadows at the time of Jesus' trial, three different people thought they recognized Peter as one of Jesus' followers and challenged him. Three times he said he didn't know him. He must afterwards have felt that with Jesus hanging on a cross, there was going to be no opportunity of talking to Jesus about his failure and that his guilt would be with him forever.

He was wrong about that and surely amazed that when they did meet on the occasion we've just heard about, Jesus made him the leader of the remaining disciples. Apparently his failure was no barrier to this because his love of Jesus outweighed any other drawback he might have.

Many caregivers feel guilty that they frequently fail the one they're caring for. They're also aware of inner feelings—frustration, resentment, disappointment—they feel guilty about having.

Marianne Talbot admits to these and links this guilt with love. If you love someone, she suggests, you're likely to feel guilty that you haven't cared for them as well as you'd like. Our guilt is in a sense a sign of the depth of love we feel. But it can also undermine the quality of our loving.

For one thing, it makes us see criticism where there is none. Peter's love had been such that he did risk going to where the trial was being held. Perhaps it was this that Jesus was picking up on in the conversation in our reading. His question to Peter, "Do you love me more than these (others)?" may have been a hint by Jesus that perhaps his love was greater than the others. He did after all go to the courtyard when nine of the other disciples simply vanished. But Peter's slightly defensive reply, "You know I do," suggests that what perhaps Jesus intended as a compliment was interpreted by Peter as criticism. His own sense of failure stopped him hearing appreciation.

This is only one of a number of ways in which guilt shuts us down. It can become so much part of our psyche that it displaces the sense we should have of our competence. It eats away at our self-confidence. This in turn makes us less effective in our caregiving, giving us more to feel guilty about, diminishing yet more our ability to care properly, and so on in a downward spiral.

The way Jesus deals with Peter's guilt is instructive. We might have thought he would simply forgive him but, if your experience of being forgiven is anything like mine, it may help restore the relationship with the one I've hurt but it doesn't stop me feeling bad about it. What Jesus wants from Peter is a straightforward, unconditional statement of confidence in his continuing ability to love and to care. He wants Peter to bring to the surface his knowledge that he does love Jesus because that will displace his sense of failure. Three times Jesus presses him simply to say the words, "Yes, I love you" but he never does —"You know I love you," which is what he does say, doesn't have anything like the same positive feel about it.

Later in this session, we'll be exploring Cognitive Behavioral Therapy a little. Described simply, it is a technique for identifying the ways we think negatively about ourselves and replacing those thoughts with positive ones. This isn't very far from what Jesus is doing with Peter by encouraging him to assert his love. It's also similar to what Marianne Talbot says when she suggests we respond to any sense of guilt by remembering "what you are doing, instead of beating yourself up for everything else."

Sometimes the barrier to doing this, to allowing our knowledge of our love to compensate in our minds for our failures, is that we don't in fact feel loving. There are times in most loving relationships when tiredness, frustration, communication difficulties, or simply finding the other person irritating leave us having all sorts of feelings about them but love isn't one of them. And yet we think we ought to feel love and worry that we don't.

But actions are more important than feelings. There are a number of words used in the original language of the New Testament for love. The one Jesus uses in his question to Peter is agape—self-sacrificial love—and it's the word Paul uses in his description of love in 1 Corinthians. Love, Paul says there, is patient and kind. It does not dishonor others, it is not self-seeking, it is not easily angered, it keeps no record of wrongs. These are all demanding qualities but they relate to behavior not feelings.

Perhaps Jesus' choice of Peter as leader was because of his courage. Peter risked a fate like Jesus' by staying nearby after not just one but three people said they recognized him. Jesus seems to have seen this loyalty as a sign of Peter's love, which far outweighed any damage done by his disloyal words. Perhaps what matters most to the people we care for is not that we occasionally fail but that we're there for them.

Some possibilities for discussion
- Are you sensitive to criticism? Any in particular? Why?
- Is guilt an essential part of love, of taking responsibility?
- Jesus took the initiative in restoring Peter's confidence. Does it help to talk to the person you are caring for about feelings of inadequacy? If they are understanding, how does that feel? And if they're not?

Learning

Cognitive Behavioral Therapy (CBT) starts from the assumption that it's not external events that make us feel good or bad; it's our mind's evaluation of them. Often when we feel inadequate or angry, despondent or frustrated, it is because our minds are stuck in ways of thinking about ourselves which lead us to interpret events in negative ways. Our minds also produce pictures of the future and the past that affect the way we feel. Again often these visualizations are negative, leaving us feeling downcast. The art of the CBT therapist is to help their client to change the way they think and the picture they have of their future so that instead of feeling pessimistic, they feel positive.

CBT suggests that by changing the way we view our lives, confidence can replace feeling inadequate and turn a sense of constant failure into self-belief. Other theories suggest this approach is inadequate because it doesn't deal with the feelings and experiences that lie behind our actions.

If the need is there, it is possible to see a CBT-trained counselor but we can take advantage of the therapy's insights by reflecting on the following questions:
- What most feeds any negative feelings about ourselves that we have—our expectations of ourselves, other people's expectations of us, comments from the person we care for, or something else?

- If we want to change, is it enough to develop a positive rather than a negative view of ourselves?
- "When you're next overwhelmed with guilt, try congratulating yourself on your capacity for love," says Marianne Talbot. What phrases might we say to ourselves, what picture might we hold in our minds, which will make us feel positive about ourselves? As an individual think of one for yourself that you can try using in the coming days.

Preparing for the next session

Remember to reflect on the positive phrase or picture you thought of in the learning section of this session.

In the next session, we shall be exploring Carl Rogers' theory about how our attitude toward other people can help them grow. Try googling "Unconditional Positive Regard" or following the links on www.caring-together.com to find out more beforehand.

Prayers

Leader   The Lord is merciful and gracious, slow to anger and abounding in steadfast love. *(Psalm 103:8)*

Now is the time for anyone in the group to mention anything going on in their lives that they are finding difficult. When there has been time for everyone who wishes to speak, a silence follows, during which each quietly prays for the members of the group who have just spoken. Anyone who wishes to say a prayer out loud can also do so.

> Generous God,
> as we pray for each other, you meet us in our need.
> Grant us the resources we need for our caregiving
> and surround us with your love.
> **Amen.**

The Lord said to me, "My grace is sufficient for you, for power is made perfect in weakness." *(2 Corinthians 12:9)*

Now go around the group in turn and each person mention the name of someone they are caring for. Follow each mention by a long enough silence for that person to be prayed for silently by the group before the next person speaks. Then all pray together:

**Loving God,
you promise to sustain all whose lives are hard.
Grant those for whom we care
your strength and your peace.
Amen.**

**May God bless us all till we meet again.
Amen.**

To take away

Before Rabbi Zusia died, he said: "When I shall face the celestial tribunal, I shall not be asked why I was not Abraham, Jacob or Moses. I shall be asked why I was not Zusia."

Traditional Jewish story

Session 4

Why Do I Care?

In this session, we will look at some of the motives that inspire our caregiving.

Opening reflection

Listen to "Love me tender" (available to download from www.kevinmayhew.com/caring-together-download.html or from www.caring-together.com).

A prayer to say together
Loving God,
thank you for caring for us tenderly and completely,
for loving us now and that you always will.
Please give us that same commitment
in the loving we offer others.
Make our loving tender and true
that it may bring a new completeness to our lives
and to the lives of those we care for.
Amen.

Gathering

Each person should take about a minute to give their name and describe something they've enjoyed today.

Exploring

Archie Hill's stepson, Barry, was not able from birth to walk, talk, feed, or toilet himself. In a talk for the BBC in the 1970s, Archie Hill describes his feelings as he watched his wife's care for Barry.

I suppose, when she took him home and did not "put him away" as the doctors advised her to—I suppose she hoped they were wrong. He was such a beautiful baby, clean-limbed and perfectly formed. He was a dark-haired baby with brown eyes that laughed out at the world. She doted upon a miniature of perfection which would soon show the development of gross imperfection, the decay in the bud. I don't think, then, that she thought her son would be imprisoned in a wheelchair all of his life, and she a prisoner with him never able to develop her own creativities. But in her mind she wasn't tied by fetters of duty but by love. A closed world of love. So rich a world, it is beyond description. I'd never met love like this before—my ideas of love had been so shallow. What privileged few amongst us really do know what love is? We know self-love, pride-love, power-love, comfort-love, dependent-love. We know shallow-love and glitter-love, and love by many other names; we know man-woman love which, as time passes and youth with it, turns into safe and comfortable habit. There are good and rich loves, most of them; but there are different levels of love and the deepest depth of all is this closed world of love between a mother and a useless creature which was the child drawn in pain from her body into a poisoned light of day.

Some possibilities for discussion
- Is there anything in this account that rings a bell for you?
- Archie suggests his wife was "a prisoner with [her son], never able to develop her own creativities." Do you ever feel like a prisoner?
- "In her mind she wasn't tied by fetters of duty but by love." Does our caregiving sometimes feel more like duty? What difference does that make to how the caregiver feels about what

they're doing? What difference does it make to how they do it?
- Can caregiving become unhealthily possessive?

Reflecting

The sources of our caring:

Someone reads from Mark 14:3-9

> While he was at Bethany in the house of Simon the leper, as he sat at the table, a woman came with an alabaster jar of very costly ointment of nard, and she broke open the jar and poured the ointment on his head. But some were there who said to one another in anger, "Why was the ointment wasted in this way? For this ointment could have been sold for more than three hundred denarii and the money given to the poor." And they scolded her.
>
> But Jesus said, "Let her alone; why do you trouble her? She has performed a good service for me. For you always have the poor with you, and you can show kindness to them whenever you wish; but you will not always have me. She has done what she could; she has anointed my body beforehand for its burial. Truly I tell you, wherever the good news is proclaimed in the whole world, what she has done will be told in remembrance of her."

Comments

(If you would like to hear the author reading these himself please refer to www.caring-together.com)

There were probably some who thought Barry's mother was wasting her life. Here was a clever, creative, energetic young woman devoting all her time and energy to a young lad who wasn't even capable of appreciating it. Some of the diners at the home of Simon of Bethany thought what the woman did to Jesus was wasteful. But Jesus recognized value in what she did—

it gave him a sense of being appreciated and she found a way of expressing the love she felt inside her.

This ability human beings have to give of themselves in a way that seems over the top is beautiful and mysterious. Much of the time, when our caregiving just seems like a desperate struggle, it doesn't feel as though that's what we're doing. Yet just occasionally we discover in ourselves evidence of a deep well of compassion and generosity that we are willing to let others draw upon. Especially when what we are feeling is drained, we want to be able to draw from that well, and to show the same generous and self-giving love as the woman.

We don't know what it was that prompted the woman to anoint Jesus so publicly. It's often thought, and is quite likely, that it was out of gratitude to him for some word or act that had brought her emotional or physical healing. But it might have been something much less identifiable—maybe it wasn't anything Jesus had said or done, just that something in him drew forth something in her. Perhaps she herself didn't even know why she did it. Sometimes there are things we just know we have to do without being able to articulate the reason.

I imagine that will be true of many of us as we ask ourselves why we care. The natural ties that bind families and neighbors may well feature prominently among our replies. Some will feel their caregiving is a way of saying thank you, either to the person they are caring for, or to God for the life they've been given, or both.

Love is often part of the reason. Sometimes though, it doesn't feel as though it is. As you were perhaps thinking about a few moments ago, there are likely to be times when our foremost feeling in our caregiving is duty not love. The danger then is that we might feel that's not how it should be and feel guilty. Guilt can be brought on by other feelings too—feelings of frustration or impatience, even that inner voice which echoes those external critics who might be saying of us: what a waste. If that happens, it's important that we don't punish ourselves. It's not how we feel that counts but what we do. When Jesus was asked to define love, in this case of a neighbor, he told the story of the Good Samaritan, which says nothing at all about how the Samaritan *felt*. It was *what he did* in going the extra mile for the person who'd been mugged that qualified his actions as loving.

Another response we might make to the question "Why do I care?" is that we like how it makes us feel. Sometimes it's the good opinion of others, who admire our generous self-giving, that makes us feel good; sometimes it's more internal—we just feel pleased with ourselves. I don't think there's anything wrong with that motivation. What matters is that the desire for that positive feeling about ourselves doesn't become more important than meeting the needs of the person we care for. We can find ourselves focusing too much on those aspects of our caregiving that make *us* feel good, or tend too much toward the parts of our caregiving that will be publicly noticed. Then an unhealthy selfishness enters our caregiving.

There's a reason some psychologists come up with to explain some kinds of caregiving. None of us, they say, received the amount of love and attention we craved as babies. As we grew up, the effects of this deficiency were partly minimized in a healthy growth toward maturity. But in most of us, to varying degrees, there remain vestiges of the belief we developed in those early years that this was our fault—we weren't lovable enough to attract the love we wanted. So in adulthood we continue the attempt started then to make ourselves more lovable. Part of this is a deep-seated and powerful motivation toward anything that will make us liked. Looking after other people, at least on the face of it, is a sure-fire way of attracting their and other people's approval. It also makes us feel good because it suggests to us we do deserve to be loved.

Was this why the woman was so extravagant in her affection

for Jesus? She wanted his love? Is this part of what drives our caregiving? A cynical viewpoint, some will say, yet true to some extent of most of us who are caregivers. Just being aware of the possibility enables us to check occasionally whether our caregiving is becoming selfish. More likely perhaps, the woman showed her love for Jesus because he had broken through her barrier against believing she was fundamentally lovable. He had made her feel loved. When we come to believe that we are lovable and let ourselves be loved, not for what we do but because of who we are, then our loving for others is more likely to have the generous, overflowing quality hers did.

Some possibilities for discussion
- Why do you think the woman did what she did? What inspires you in your caregiving?
- Archie Hill talked about self-love, pride-love, power-love, comfort-love, dependent-love, shallow-love, and glitter-love. Do any of these play a part in what we offer those we care for?
- Are there any compensations we experience for any sacrifice we may be making?

Learning

The phrase "Unconditional Positive Regard" was first used by the psychologist Carl Rogers and describes the attitude toward others that is most likely to enable them to grow. Many people feel highly critical of themselves and easily pick up criticism in what others say to them. This stunts their development as human beings. To counteract this, it's helpful to offer committed support and complete acceptance of the person—though not necessarily of their behavior.

Some possibilities for discussion
- Discuss the challenges of such an approach to your situations, especially where the behavior of the person being cared for makes such acceptance difficult.
- Talk together about the difficulty of distinguishing between accepting someone as a person and accepting their actions.
- Within this group how would putting into practice Unconditional Positive Regard affect the way we behave toward each other?

Preparing for the next session

In the next session, we shall be learning about a theory which offers insights into how we communicate with each other. Try googling "Myers Briggs basics," explore www.myersbriggs.org or follow the links on www.caring-together.com.

Prayers

Leader The steadfast love of the Lord never ceases, his mercies never come to an end; they are new every morning. *(Lamentations 3:22-23)*

Now is the time for anyone in the group to mention anything going on in their lives that they are finding difficult. When there has been time for everyone who wishes to speak, a silence follows, during which each quietly prays for the members of the group who have just spoken. Anyone who wishes to say a prayer out loud can also do so.

> Generous God,
> as we pray for each other, you meet us in our need.
> Grant us the resources we need for our caregiving
> and surround us with your love.
> **Amen.**

> Cast your burden on the Lord, and he will sustain you. *(Psalm 55:22)*

Now go around the group in turn and each person mention the name of someone they are caring for. Follow each mention by a long enough silence for that person to be prayed for silently by the group before the next person speaks. Then all pray together:

> **Loving God,**
> **you promise to sustain all whose lives are hard.**
> **Grant those for whom we care**
> **your strength and your peace.**
> **Amen.**
>
> **May God bless us all till we meet again.**
> **Amen.**

To take away

An old man was walking along a beach in Mexico after an unusually strong spring storm. The beach was covered with dying starfish tossed up by the waves, and he was tossing them back into the water one by one. A visitor saw this and came up to him. "What are you doing?" "I'm trying to help these starfish," the old man replied. "But there are tens of thousands of them washed up on these beaches. Throwing a handful back won't make any difference," protested the visitor. "It'll make a difference to this one," the old man replied as he tossed another starfish into the ocean.

Jack Kornfield, *After the Ecstasy, the Laundry*

Session 5
Listening

In this session we will explore the task of listening and what can sometimes stop us from doing so.

Opening reflection
Listen to "Let's call the whole thing off" (available to download from www.kevinmayhew.com/caring-together-download.html or from www.caring-together.com).

A prayer to say together
Creative God,
you have made us all different.
Thank you
for the wide variety in human personality and character.
We're sorry that sometimes our differences
create tensions between us
and make it hard for us to listen to each other.
Grant us attentiveness to really listen to those we care for
that we may respond to their needs in the way they want;
and courage to go on listening
when what they're saying is painful to hear
that they may feel stronger
because we're sharing some of their pain.
In the name of your Son, Jesus.
Amen.

Gathering
Each person should take about a minute to give their name and say what kind of music, if any, they enjoy listening to.

Exploring

Ken Wilber shared with his wife Treya her journey through cancer to death. In his book *Grace and Grit* he shares his own reflections on that time and on his wider experience as a psychologist and cancer sufferer himself. Into the book are incorporated extracts from Treya's diary.

> Treya:
>
> Most people who are ill are undergoing a great deal of stress dealing with it. Their needs should be respected, the limits they suggest should at least be considered. Not that I don't believe in healthy confrontation at the right moment, for I certainly do. What I object to is people theorising about me and not bothering to ask me what my thoughts on myself and this illness are. I have had cancer. I feel bad enough about this, about the threat to my life, about the surgery and treatments I have had to undergo. It has been frightening. I have been unkind to myself (by asking myself what I might have done to bring this on myself). I do not need you to be unkind to me too. I need you to understand, to be gentle, not to theorise about me behind my back. I need you to ask me, not to tell me. I need you to try to understand what this must feel like, just a little, to put yourself in my place and hopefully treat me more kindly than I sometimes treat myself.

> Ken:
>
> Over the years I've talked to a lot of people who have cancer, many who have recently been diagnosed. At first I wasn't sure what to say. It was easiest to talk about my own experiences as a cancer patient, but I soon saw that often that was not what a particular person needed to hear. The only way I could discover how to help someone

was by listening. Only when I heard what they were trying to say could I get a sense of what they needed, of the issues they were confronting at that time, of the kind of help that would really help at that specific moment. Since people go through many different phases during the course of an illness that can be as persistent and unpredictable as cancer, learning to listen to what they need is especially important.

Some possibilities for discussion
- Is there anything in this account that rings a bell for you?
- Treya asks for allowance to be made for the fact that she's suffering. In what ways, if at all, would you treat someone differently because of what they are going through?
- Treya asks that others put themselves in her place. Share experiences of trying to put yourself in the shoes of the person you are caring for.
- Treya asks to be consulted about what concerns her. When might caregivers be tempted not to do that? What's it like when such consultation isn't possible?

Reflecting

Listening to pain:

Someone reads from John 19:25b-27

Meanwhile, standing near the cross of Jesus were his mother, and his mother's sister, Mary, the wife of Clopas, and Mary Magdalene. When Jesus saw his mother and the disciple whom he loved standing beside her, he said to his mother, "Woman, here is your son." Then he said to the disciple, "Here is your mother." And from that hour the disciple took her into his own home.

Comments

(If you would like to hear the author reading these himself please refer to www.caring-together.com)

Really being alongside someone in their pain is an enormous challenge. Barbara Want in her book about the early death of her husband Nick Clarke describes angrily how people she met in the weeks following his death simply wouldn't mention the subject. And if *she* did, they changed the topic as quickly as they could. People simply didn't want to hear her pain. We may well have had similar experiences. I've often sensed as I've responded truthfully to the question "How's your wife?" that the point of the question was to show a superficial concern, not really to hear about and so share some of the pain.

The incident we've just read about offers a different model. Unlike the disciples who, with the exception of John, were nowhere to be seen, Jesus' mother and two other women stayed to be with him for his final hours. The words of the thirteenth-century poem about this, "Stabat Mater', suggests that this moment fulfilled the prophecy of Simeon at Jesus' birth that a sword would pierce Mary's heart:

> Through her heart, his sorrow sharing,
> all his bitter anguish bearing,
> now at length the sword has passed.

The metaphor of a sword passing through us is not a bad one to describe the experience of being alongside those we care for. Their physical or mental pain, their frustration or physical restrictions, can make watching them struggle or suffer agonizing. There may be occasions when the agony is too much for us. Then we need to do the equivalent of the disciples who fled. If we can't bear it, we need to learn to protect ourselves if we are going to be able to continue our practical caregiving.

Much of the time, though, we will want to listen, hard though it is. It's particularly difficult when the one we care for isn't capable of straightforward verbal communication. Having to rely on picking up signals, on body language, or on plain guesswork, is especially hard. But even when we want to listen and there is communication, there are times when we're not fully responsive to the pain being expressed.

Sometimes we may offer over-hasty reassurance. There's a difficult balance to be struck here. When those we care for are feeling low, they are sometimes incapable of keeping that distance from their situation that would enable them to see where there are positive signs. With that little extra detachment of the caregiver, we can sometimes point these out. Unrealistic encouragement cuts no ice but specific, even quite small, possibilities, can be reassuring. But coming in with these too soon can be a way of defending ourselves against the pain of hearing about feelings of despondency and despair. These are often all too real and it can be helpful for the person experiencing them to express them, however hard it may be for us to listen. Experience can give us the ability to know at what point to intervene with a more positive outlook but what's important is that that timing is not chosen to save *us* pain but for what we see as most beneficial for the person we care for.

Of course, the majority of those we care for will be well aware that it is hard to listen to someone describing their struggles. Sometimes this means that they won't talk about it. They button their lips and keep it to themselves. What's more, because of our different personalities, we may not realize how much talking the person we're caring for needs to do. They might need to share what they're feeling more than we would; they may be more likely than we would be to feel they're boring us when they do. Because we wouldn't need to talk as much, we may not realize that the one we care for is holding back and needs encouragement to talk.

It may of course be the other way around—we need to talk more than the one we're caring for. If so, we may not understand why they don't talk more and so try to push them to do so inappropriately. Or we may be tempted to use them as listeners to us more than is appropriate. The material in the learning section of this session is designed to help us be more aware of these and similar temperamental differences.

If we're a different gender from the one we care for, that can also lead to differences that may make listening difficult. To summarize a huge topic, women often communicate on an emotional level of relationship and connection, on feelings first, rather than fact. Men on the other hand tend to assess the status of an issue and look for a solution by reasoning. Here, as with temperamental differences, it's easy to stop listening because the topic isn't being approached in the way *we* would approach it.

What Mary stood there and listened to as Jesus expressed his pain on the cross must have been very difficult to hear. "My God, my God, why have you forsaken me?" But there were also words of love as Jesus invited his mother and his best friend to care for each other after his death. Among the things the people we care for say that are hard to hear, there will also, if we are fortunate, be words of encouragement for us, words of gratitude and appreciation. Let's not miss those. When they come, let's resist any temptation to brush them off and let's make sure that we really hear them.

Some possibilities for discussion
- What's hard about being alongside pain?
- Of the things the person you care for expresses, which are hard to hear and respond to?
- What do you do if you can't listen any longer?

- If the one you care for is able to communicate effectively, how helpful to them do you think it is to talk about what they're going through? Do they need encouraging to do this?

Learning

Katharine Briggs and Isabel Myers developed a test based on Carl Jung's ideas about personality types. This is important because one of the difficulties in really listening to someone else is that they will probably have a different personality type from you and so have needs you might not recognize because you haven't got them.

To make best use of this Myers-Briggs theory, there's no substitute for taking the test with a properly qualified practitioner but, even without that, it's possible to identify the personality types that fit most closely with you and those with the person you care for. We are all a mixture of the different types and therefore shouldn't overly label ourselves or others but it's worth being aware of some of the types Myers-Briggs identify. The following is my own chart and shouldn't be taken as more than a very simplistic summary of the theory. But to give an example, this book's author is (based on this chart rather than the official test) ESFP, i.e. he's more of an Extrovert than an Introvert (though he doesn't like too much external stimulation), more Sensing than iNtuitive (that word isn't used here entirely according to its normal usage), more Feeling than Thinking, and more Perceiving than Judging (though he does like to be in control).

Type		Possible Irritants
Introvert—looks inwards, reflective, one thing at a time, needs time to think, seeks escape from constant external stimulation.	**Extrovert**—looks outwards, active, speaks to find out what they think, likes external stimulation.	• **E** may want much more conversation and background TV/Radio. • **I** may not realize **E** is only trying out an idea; it's not the final word on the subject.
Sensing—very conscious of environment, capacity to enjoy life as it is, likes instructions to be exact and follows them.	**iNtuition**—environment less important, likely to have clear idea how things might be better, capable of apparently illogical jumps.	• **N** more content with untidiness. • **S** unhappy with **N**'s desire to be always changing things. • **S** can't see how **N** reached a particular decision.
Thinking—choices based on logical criteria, truth more important than tact, looks at issues from outside, decisions either true or false.	**Feeling**—choices perfectly rational but based on personal/social needs more than logic, decisions either good or bad.	• **F** thinks **T** is too critical. • **T** thinks **F** is being illogical. • **F** thinks **T** is too detached.
Perceiving—likes open-endedness, tolerant, experience-orientated.	**Judging**—likes structure, anxious in uncertainty, likes to be in control.	• **P** doesn't keep to **J**'s timetable. • **J** wants to hurry **P** into making a decision.

Some possibilities for discussion
- Share any of the findings of those who've had time to research this theory or who have experienced the Myers-Briggs test previously.

- Share with each other which of the two types in each row of the first two columns you feel most describes you and which most describes the person you care for.
- Do any of the suggested "irritants" apply to the relationship? Are there others?

Preparing for the next session

In the next session, we shall be talking about Keat's theory of Negative Capability. More information can be found by googling "Negative Capability" or following the links on www.caring-together.com.

Prayers

Leader God is our refuge and strength, a very present help in trouble. Therefore we will not fear. *(Psalm 46:1-2)*

Now is the time for anyone in the group to mention anything going on in their lives that they are finding difficult. When there has been time for everyone who wishes to speak, a silence follows, during which each quietly prays for the members of the group who have just spoken. Anyone who wishes to say a prayer out loud can also do so.

> Generous God,
> as we pray for each other, you meet us in our need.
> Grant us the resources we need for our caregiving
> and surround us with your love.
> **Amen.**
>
> God says: "As a mother comforts her child, so I will comfort you." *(Isaiah 66:13)*

Now go around the group in turn and each person mention the name of someone they are caring for. Follow each mention by a long enough silence for that person to be prayed for silently by the group before the next person speaks. Then all pray together:

> **Loving God,**
> **you promise to sustain all whose lives are hard.**
> **Grant those for whom we care**
> **your strength and your peace.**
> **Amen.**
>
> **May God bless us all till we meet again.**
> **Amen.**

To take away

The doctor bent over the lifeless figure in the bed. Then he straightened up and said, "I'm sorry to say that your husband is no more, my dear." A feeble sound of protest came from the lifeless figure in the bed: "No, I'm still alive." "Hold your tongue," said the woman. "The doctor knows better than you."

Anthony de Mello, *The Heart of the Enlightened*

Session 6

Trying to Understand

In this session, we will look at whether there are any explanations for suffering that work and how to handle it if there aren't.

Opening reflection
Listen to "If I ruled the world" (available to download from www.kevinmayhew.com/caring-together-download.html or from www.caring-together.com).

A prayer to say together
Compassionate God,
it's you who rules the world
yet we can't believe the suffering in it is what you want.
Help us to go on trusting that you know what you're doing
and to find meaning, even in the pain.
May our dreams for a better world
inspire us to keep going when life is tough
and the knowledge that you are with us in our struggles
give us hope.
Amen.

Gathering
Each person should take about a minute to give their name and to tell the group their earliest memory.

Exploring
The theologian and Methodist Minister Frances Young has a son, Arthur, who has profound learning and physical disabilities.

He is totally dependent for all his everyday functions, such as feeding, washing, dressing, and mobility. Here she describes how this affected her relationship with God.

> My experience was of an internal blank where God should have been. I had no hope for the future. Despair was lodged deep down inside, even if for the most part I got on with life and joked and played with the kids, and lectured in theology, and researched and wrote, passed for a Christian and went to church. Occasionally I would wrestle with meaningless prayer to a blank wall . . .
>
> For years I found holding onto faith profoundly difficult. God seemed absent. But then one day, as I got up from a chair to go and do some household chore, I suddenly heard a voice, as it were: "It makes no difference to me whether you believe in me or not!" It was meaningful at all kinds of levels: for one thing, I was absolved of responsibility for deciding about God, for God no longer depended on me for existence—God just "is", independent of what I thought or felt . . .
>
> The need to let go of pre-occupations and anxieties, to journey into the unknown, to accept the utter transcendence and incomprehensibility of God, allowed me a renewal of faith, and soon afterwards a sense of vocation in which Arthur became a central part of my ministry. Overall, my journey has involved a profound shifting away from . . . the anguished questioning of a Job, to a sense that through the wilderness of coping with Arthur I have had privileged access to a deeper sense of meaning and value—indeed, the deepest truths of Christian theology. It is in the desert that you grow, pruned and purged so that the fruits of the Spirit can germinate when the rains come.

Some possibilities for discussion
- Is there anything in this account that rings a bell for you?
- Frances Young's deep despair was hidden behind an outward normality. Do you hide how you are really feeling?
- Frances Young "passed" for a Christian. Do you sometimes have a sense of "going through the motions" in relation to church going, prayer, or other religious practices?
- Frances Young's attitude changed profoundly when the pressure she felt to believe was removed. Do you feel under pressure to believe? If so, where's it coming from?

Reflecting

The question why:

Someone reads from John 9:1-5

> As he walked along, he saw a man blind from birth. His disciples asked him, "Rabbi, who sinned, this man or his parents, that he was born blind?" Jesus answered, "Neither this man nor his parents sinned; he was born blind so that God's works might be revealed in him. We must work the works of him who sent me while it is day; night is coming when no one can work. As long as I am in the world, I am the light of the world."

Comments

(If you would like to hear the author reading these himself please refer to www.caring-together.com)

In the '60s musical of the same name, Pickwick is mistaken for an election candidate. The song we heard at the beginning—"If I ruled the world"—is his response to a request for his manifesto. The kind of world it portrays is the kind we'd all like—a world of sunshine and smiles. Why is it not like that?

This was the question in the disciples' minds when they

tackled Jesus on the causes of a man's blindness. It was probably an even more sensitive issue for the man's parents. It was they who had had to provide the extra care their child needed and it can be in the day-to-day process of caregiving that the question becomes most acute.

In this passage Jesus immediately rejects one answer to the question of why there's suffering. Suffering is not a judgment or a punishment. It's a very deeply embedded instinct to link pain and punishment (interestingly the words have the same Latin root—*poena*) but the man was not blind, Jesus insisted, because of anyone's sin. Feeling guilty about it is not an appropriate way of reacting to suffering.

A more helpful reaction is based on the idea that though suffering can be terrible, good can come out of it. Frances Young implies in the passages of her writings we looked at just now that her experience of parenting and being with Arthur has helped her grow. She said, "It is in the desert that you grow, pruned and purged so that the fruits of the Spirit can germinate when the rains come." Many people bear witness to the fact that their suffering has strengthened them . . . but do such positive effects justify the terrible pain and the devastating trauma some people suffer?

The biblical book that is most relevant to the question of suffering is Job. His friends come up with all sorts of explanations as to why he lost his family, his livelihood, and his health. In the end though, Job simply accepts that he can't understand it. God asserts the power with which he created the whole world and reminds Job of his limited place within it, "Where were you when I laid the foundations of the earth?" "I have uttered what I did not understand," replies Job, "things too wonderful for me, which I did not know." His response is echoed by Frances Young when she says that she learned "to accept the utter transcendence and incomprehensibility of God." In the end, there is no answer to the problem that human minds can fathom. For some this makes it impossible for them to believe. But others are content to accept the limitations of our understanding and to go on trusting.

The basis for that trust is to be found in Jesus' reply to the question in the reading. What he says doesn't explain the man's blindness but it puts it into the context of Jesus' own suffering. "The night is coming," says Jesus. He's looking ahead to his experience of darkness, when he will enter into the depths of human suffering and pain. He sees this as doing "the work of him who sent me" and it leads to the resurrection, a powerful culmination of that work of God's. There is no *reason* for the blind man's suffering but there might be a *purpose*, a value in it, if, like his own suffering, it becomes a means by which "the work of God is displayed."

There is no answer to the question "Why?" When I think about my wife's constant pain, about the many gifts she has which are going to waste because of it, I feel angry. It seems so unfair and meaningless. Yet it's only one of millions of similar situations. I blame God yet I'm also convinced he loves us so I just have to live with that dilemma.

But what does comfort me is the knowledge that Christ promises to support us. I would echo the words of a caregiver who has helped me with this book. "When things are really bad," she wrote, "and there feels nothing more I can do, I pray and pass the care of [the one she cares for] onto God—and I've found that very helpful." God may have created a world in which suffering exists and is randomly distributed but, through Jesus, he also came and shared in it. He knows firsthand what it's like to be on the receiving end of injustice and pain. I find it helps to know that when I seek God's support during hard times, the one I'm calling upon has himself experienced suffering. It's usually the case, isn't it, that there's a deeper authenticity in the support offered by someone we know has been there. Because Jesus shared our suffering, he also understands it.

We won't easily get our minds around the philosophical and theological issues raised by the suffering of the one we care for—or by our own suffering. We can only try and salvage something creative from it and hope that somehow its meaning reveals itself in the experience of it.

Some possibilities for discussion
- If you "ruled the world" would suffering be part of it?
- How has your experience of suffering changed you?
- Does it help to be told that Christ shares in our suffering? Do you think it's true?

Learning

John Keats' theory of "Negative Capability" was his response to aspects of life he couldn't understand. Writing in one of his letters about what makes a great poet, Keats suggested it was the ability to be "in uncertainties, Mysteries, doubts without any irritable reaching after fact & reason." Unlike his fellow Romantic poets, Coleridge and Wordsworth, he didn't want always to be seeking explanation and certainty but felt instead that we should "open our leaves like a flower and be passive and receptive." His view was that "the sense of Beauty overcomes every other consideration, or rather obliterates every other consideration."

Some possibilities for discussion
- Job, Frances Young, and Keats all seem to recommend an attitude of openness toward creation. How could you put yourself and/or the person you care for into closer touch with the natural world? Why not try out any ideas you come up with during the coming days?

- Are you comfortable living with "uncertainties"?
- Share any experiences you've had of finding beauty in the way someone suffering or disabled responds to it.

Preparing for the next session

In the next session, we shall be exploring a way of thinking about anger suggested by the "Human Givens" theory. Follow the links on www.caring-together.com. There's also information at http://www.hgi.org.uk/archive/anger.htm and on the page (called "What are the Human Givens?") that you are directed to at the bottom of that article.

Prayers

Leader The Lord is good to all, and his compassion is over all that he has made. *(Psalm 145:9)*

Now is the time for anyone in the group to mention anything going on in their lives that they are finding difficult. When there has been time for everyone who wishes to speak, a silence follows, during which each quietly prays for the members of the group who have just spoken. Anyone who wishes to say a prayer out loud can also do so.

> Generous God,
> as we pray for each other, you meet us in our need.
> Grant us the resources we need for our caregiving
> and surround us with your love.
> **Amen.**

> The father of the child cried out, "I believe; help my unbelief!" . . . Jesus took him [the boy] by the hand and lifted him up, and he was able to stand. *(Mark 9:24, 27)*

Now go around the group in turn and each person mention the name of someone they are caring for. Follow each mention by a long enough silence for that person to be prayed for silently by the group before the next person speaks. Then all pray together:

> **Loving God,**
> **you promise to sustain all whose lives are hard.**
> **Grant those for whom we care**
> **your strength and your peace.**
> **Amen.**
>
> **May God bless us all till we meet again.**
> **Amen.**

To take away

In *Mister God this is Anna,* the author describes conversations with six-year-old Anna.

"Questions are in boxes," said Anna, "the answers only fit the size of the box."

"That's difficult; go on a bit."

"The questions get to the edge and then stop. It's like a prison."

"I expect we're all in some sort of prison."

She shook her head. "No, Mister God wouldn't do that."

"I suppose not. What's the answer then?"

"Let Mister God be. He lets us be."

"Don't we?"

"No. We put Mister God into little boxes."

"Surely we don't do that?"

"Yes, all the time. Because we don't really love him. We got to let Mister God be free. That's what love is."

Session 7

Anger

In this session, we will explore the kinds of anger caregivers might be susceptible to and how to deal with them.

Opening reflection
Listen to "Pack up your troubles in your old kit bag" (available to download from www.kevinmayhew.com/caring-together-download.html or from www.caring-together.com). A "lucifer," mentioned in the song, was a popular make of match.

A prayer to say together
Generous God,
you understand the anger life often brings.
It sometimes feels like a burden to be carried.
Remind us that you take such troubles
and free us from their grip.
Help us not to deny our anger nor to give in to it
but to accept it as an inevitable part of our lives.
So that when we smile,
it's the smile of one who has learned to let their anger
be part of their onward journey.
Through Jesus Christ our Lord.
Amen.

Gathering
Each person should take about a minute to give their name and tell the group what makes them cross.

Exploring

Nick Clarke, former presenter of the BBC radio show "World at One," died of cancer in 2006. His widow, Barbara Want, who was left with two small children, has written about his dying and her bereavement in her book, *Why not me?*. Here she's writing about the time the diagnosis began to sink in.

> At around this time I began to be visited by an unwelcome emotion which I find hard to admit to. Anger came over me in waves, and I couldn't fight it. I was angry at what was happening to us, to me, to the boys. Angry about what lay ahead, whatever it might be. Angry that I couldn't do anything to make things better. And angry with myself about the anger I felt towards Nick for taking us all to this terrible place. For the truth was that from the moment it became clear that Nick was seriously ill, I hadn't felt drawn into a struggle which united us, but rather into one that divided us by the very different nature of the separate battles we faced. Nick was a patient facing his own mortality. I was a carer, fighting not just for his survival, but also for mine and the boys', and for what we held most dear —our happy and secure life with a man we loved to bits. And I was very, very scared.
>
> I still find it hard to think about my feelings at that time. They leave me with a bad taste in my mouth. They were, and are, unpalatable. Nick seemed to understand how I felt, though we never discussed it, and his lack of self-pity, combined with the stoicism and strength he showed, made me yet more disappointed—at myself. But however I raged, my love for Nick and the pain of seeing what he was enduring never left me. It almost exploded out of my heart. And I have no doubt that his own battle was driven by his extraordinary capacity for love—for all of us.

Some possibilities for discussion

- Is there anything in this account that rings a bell for you?
- What makes you angry? Is it an "unwelcome emotion"?
- Barbara Want says the anger she felt against her dying husband was particularly hard to admit to. Is anger at the person they're caring for something caregivers sometimes feel?
- One reason she felt angry was her awareness there was nothing she could do to make things better. She was also "very scared." What kinds of powerlessness and fear do caregivers feel? Is anger one response to those feelings? What other reactions do they evoke?

Reflecting

Anger and rage:

Someone reads from Mark 11:15-19

> Then they came to Jerusalem. And [Jesus] entered the temple and began to drive out those who were selling and those who were buying in the temple, and he overturned the tables of the money-changers and the seats of those who sold doves; and he would not allow anyone to carry anything through the temple. He was teaching and saying, "Is it not written, 'My house will be called a house of prayer for all the nations'? But you have made it a den of robbers." And when the chief priests and the scribes heard it, they kept looking for a way to kill him; for they were afraid of him, because the whole crowd was spellbound by his teaching. And when evening came, Jesus and his disciples went out of the city.

Comments

(If you would like to hear the author reading these himself please refer to www.caring-together.com)

Most of us learned in early childhood that if you show anger, have a tantrum, you risk feeling as though love is being withdrawn by your parents. Many Christians have been imbued, often from childhood, with the idea that Christianity and anger are not compatible. So we find it very hard to be angry. Clearly for Jesus though there's nothing profane about it. Whereas for him oppression and exploitation were completely wrong in that holy place, the Temple, he seems to have felt it appropriate to express his anger there. There are also some relevant words in Ephesians: "Be angry but do not sin; do not let the sun go down on your anger" (4:26). Anger is encouraged as something that must not be allowed to build up and should be appropriately expressed.

People have very different ways of expressing their anger. Recent research suggests the differences don't relate to gender —men and women are equally likely to keep quiet in the workplace, but screaming, or talking it out, or even getting violent in the privacy of a home is equally likely from either sex. Because of this it's quite possible that the person we care for occasionally gets angry in the privacy of home. Perhaps their frustration becomes too much and they take it out on the one closest to them. For others though the opposite happens. Precisely because they feel so dependent on the one caring for them, the person being cared for feels unable to risk losing them by being angry with them. Their anger, expressed or suppressed, is one of the hardest things someone trying to care for them has to deal with.

What Barbara Want describes though is the anger she felt as she cared for her husband. She put it down to feeling scared. It's a feeling many caregivers have. We're afraid in case a situation arises that we can't cope with or are scared of making a mistake that might have serious consequences for the one we care for; we're frightened for them that a sudden deterioration or accident might destroy their fragile ability to keep up their spirits.

Or we feel frustrated by situations where we feel messed around or not listened to by public institutions. The sense of powerlessness frightens us and makes us feel angry.

One theory about how we respond to this feeling of being frightened or threatened includes two possible reactions. They are flight or fight. Flight can involve physical removal from the situation but it might also entail pushing the feelings away by trying not to think about them; we deny their power with phrases like "must not grumble." Because this doesn't actually deal with the fear, it leaves beneath the surface feelings that are going to affect our behavior whether we like it or not. It's quite an effort keeping our fear under wraps and, among other things, doing so often stops us thinking straight so we're not so good at communicating.

More creative is the "fight" response. This usually takes the form of rage. One contemporary psychotherapist, Sue Parker-Hall, helpfully distinguishes between rage and anger. Rage, she says, developed in us in our childhood as a defense mechanism when our basic needs were not being met. It is the only way open to a baby or infant to fight back when their survival feels under threat. We feel it as adults—a sudden welling up of infuriation or frustration. Perhaps a misunderstanding with the person we care for, a sudden feeling of being taken for granted, a time-wasting interaction with an outside institution, even a mistake we've made that makes us angry with ourselves—any of these and many other similar situations can make us feel physically agitated. Barbara Want's comments describe well the fear that leads to rage. She says she felt "angry about what lay ahead, whatever it might be, angry that I couldn't do anything to make things better, and angry with myself about the anger I felt towards Nick for taking us all to this terrible place." This kind of rage uses up a great deal of energy but there are ways of learning to handle it that we'll look at later in today's learning section.

Anger, on the other hand, says Sue Parker-Hall, originated in the more creative process by which we separated from our parents. It's a positive, necessary emotion that plays an essential and energizing part in us becoming ourselves. It was anger, not rage, which Jesus displayed in the Temple. The abuse of the temple rituals he saw there provoked a passion in him which gave powerful energy to his actions. It's the kind of passion we might feel as we see the one we love and care for struggling in ways that most people don't have to or see our own lives being restricted because we are committed to caring for them. It's what I think Barbara Want was experiencing when she said, "I was angry at what was happening to us, to me, to the boys." This kind of anger can be valuable if we can learn to channel that passion into creative outlets. If we're not afraid of the power of those feelings, they can give renewed energy to our caregiving.

Learning to distinguish between these two similar but very different emotions requires that we review each situation in which we feel this kind of agitation emerging so that we can learn to distinguish between them. But it could make quite a difference to us if we were able to stop wasting energy by being enraged and let the passion of our anger turn into new and creative energy.

Some possibilities for discussion
- Discuss the distinction between rage and anger. Is it helpful?
- What are the best ways of dealing with rage—your own and that of the one you care for?
- Share any experiences you may have of anger being channelled creatively.

Learning

The Human Givens approach works from the assumption that every human being has a set of needs and, if they are born healthy, they also have the internal mechanisms, their Human Givens, to ensure they are met. Anger can occur when that balance is not working effectively. In the short term, the kind of fear or panic that we have seen to be the source of much of our rage is best dealt with by incorporating various calming techniques into our daily routine. Some of them are well known—concentrating on breathing, clenching and then relaxing muscles (especially the fists), practising mindfulness (focusing intently on a simple task). The approach also emphasizes the importance of sleep and exercise.

In the longer term, we can prevent the anger that arises when our needs are not met by making sure they are. The website (http://www.hgi.org.uk/archive/anger.htm) that was suggested in the last session gives lists of our basic needs and of the resources we have to meet them. Here are some examples, particularly ones relevant to caregivers:

Needs:
- Attention (to give and receive it)—a form of nutrition.
- Feeling part of a wider community.
- Privacy—opportunity to reflect and consolidate experience.
- Meaning and purpose—which come from being stretched in what we do and think.

Resources:
- The ability to build rapport, empathize and connect with others.
- Emotions and instinct.
- An observing self—that part of us that can step back, be more objective, and be aware of itself as a unique center of awareness.

Some possibilities for discussion
- What techniques do you find help you maintain your equilibrium in stressful situations?
- Which needs or resources from the lists above or from those on the website are you neglecting?
- We've been focusing on when *we* feel angry. Share thoughts about strategies for helping the person you care for deal with any anger they may be feeling.

Preparing for the next session

In the next session, we shall be talking about a book entitled *The Practice of the Presence of God* by Brother Lawrence. It's quite short and can be read in its entirety on the internet. To do so, follow the links on www.caring-together.com.

Prayers

Leader Nothing "in all creation, will be able to separate us from the love of God in Christ Jesus our Lord." *(Romans 8:39)*

Now is the time for anyone in the group to mention anything going on in their lives that they are finding difficult. When there has been time for everyone who wishes to speak, a silence follows, during which each quietly prays for the members of the group who have just spoken. Anyone who wishes to say a prayer out loud can also do so.

> Generous God,
> as we pray for each other, you meet us in our need.
> Grant us the resources we need for our caregiving
> and surround us with your love.
> **Amen.**

> Do not worry about anything, but in everything by prayer and supplication with thanksgiving let your requests be made known to God. And the peace of God, which surpasses all understanding, will guard your hearts and your minds in Christ Jesus. *(Philippians 4:6-7)*

Now go around the group in turn and each person mention the name of someone they are caring for. Follow each mention by a long enough silence for that person to be prayed for silently by the group before the next person speaks. Then all pray together:

> **Loving God,**
> **you promise to sustain all whose lives are hard.**
> **Grant those for whom we care**
> **your strength and your peace.**
> **Amen.**
>
> **May God bless us all till we meet again.**
> **Amen.**

To take away

The poem the extract below is taken from describes a three-walled room in which a raven beats himself against the walls. No amount of loving encouragement will persuade it simply to fly out by the open wall—it's made "a prison of a place which is not one at all." But when two other ravens come and make him angry by taunting him, he flies away "o'er flattened wall at once to heaven's skies" (the whole poem can be found on the internet).

> Anger it was that won him hence
> as only Anger taught him sense.
> Often my tears fall in a shower
> Because of Anger's Freeing Power.
>
> *"Anger's Freeing Power," Stevie Smith*

Session 8
Getting Support

In this session, we will share together the need to find support in our caregiving and where we might look for it.

Opening reflection
Listen to "What a wonderful world" (available to download from www.kevinmayhew.com/caring-together-download.html or from www.caring-together.com).

A prayer to say together
Wonderful God,
the world you created and the people in it
inspire us by their beauty.
Thank you for all the support we receive in our lives.
Give us the wisdom to welcome it
when friends reach out their hands to us in love
and to be open to others' encouragement and kindness.
In the name of your Son, Jesus.
Amen.

Gathering
Each person should take about a minute to remind the group of their name and describe a particular friend and why they are special.

Exploring
Grace Sheppard, wife of the former Bishop of Liverpool and England cricketer David Sheppard, has written in *Living with Dying* about her husband's final illness.

Around this time in David's journey with cancer, when we knew that the end was in sight, I decided to look for [someone to be a soul friend]. After some time, I found one. I chose to consult a priest slightly removed from my own church who knew and respected David. He agreed to see me on a regular basis. I asked him to help me to let David go. It was essential to my spiritual health and general well-being to be able to give account and to unburden systematically to someone who could listen and observe from a more detached position, and who could discern whether or not I was being authentic or whether I was putting on an act. There is a place for putting on a brave face in public, but not at the expense of facing reality in the private place. I fancy that having this safe place also saved me from the neurosis of spraying my concerns around and becoming exhausted with repeating myself, or boring people, or confused by varied advice . . . The hour I spent with him each week became a place where I could confess things I was ashamed of and where I could weep without fear of being overwhelmed with a suffocating sympathy or religiosity, or be told to pull myself together. Here I could laugh at myself and we could laugh together. These sessions continue. It has become a place of accountability on earth without judgement; a place of encouragement and insight without sentimentality; a place where I feel respected as a human being and never patronised. It is a place full of wisdom and common sense, where I can rebalance myself after particular traumas. I am helped to do my own growing up. Overall it is a safe place, a place in which God's pure love and mercy are being channelled. It is a hallowed friendship that has been a lynchpin in helping me to take each new step in the adventure of life.

Some possibilities for discussion
- Is there anything in this account that rings a bell for you?
- Grace Sheppard writes of the need to unburden. Where have you found the best such support—friends, family, fellow caregivers, fellow sufferers, soul friends? Share examples of really helpful support you have received.
- She says she was afraid of boring people with her concerns. Is that, in your experience, something to beware of or are caregivers more likely to err on the side of not sharing what's going on for them?
- With her soul friend, Grace Sheppard found opportunity for confession, weeping, laughter, encouragement, wisdom, and safety. Which of these do you feel the need of and where could you get them?

Reflecting

Friends:

Someone reads from Mark 14:32-42, 51-52

> They went to a place called Gethsemane; and [Jesus] said to his disciples, "Sit here while I pray." He took with him Peter and James and John, and began to be distressed and agitated. And he said to them, "I am deeply grieved, even to death; remain here and keep awake." And going a little farther, he threw himself on the ground and prayed that, if it were possible, the hour might pass from him. He said, "Abba, Father, for you all things are possible; remove this cup from me; yet not what I want, but what you want." He came and found them sleeping; and he said to Peter, "Simon, are you asleep? Could you not keep awake one hour? Keep awake and pray that you may not come into the time of trial; the spirit indeed is willing, but the flesh is weak." And again he went away and prayed, saying the

same words. And once more he came and found them sleeping, for their eyes were very heavy; and they did not know what to say to him. He came a third time and said to them, "Are you still sleeping and taking your rest? Enough! The hour has come. The Son of Man is betrayed into the hands of sinners. Get up, let us be going. See, my betrayer is at hand."

A certain young man was following him, wearing nothing but a linen cloth. They caught hold of him, but he left the linen cloth and ran off naked.

Comments

(If you would like to hear the author reading these himself please refer to www.caring-together.com)

Grace Sheppard chose a fairly particular form of support for herself while she was caring for her dying husband. As you've no doubt been saying to each other—hers is not everyone's cup of tea. But I would guess there has been no dispute in the group that what she got from that relationship is something we'd all find very supportive.

When Jesus chose his twelve disciples he was looking partly for people who would share with him in what lay ahead, to support him through it. In some cases, we might question his judgment. James and John were ambitious, Peter impetuous, Judas disloyal, Thomas stubborn. But each of them, in spite of their particular peccadilloes, had something to offer him. Among the friends we've chosen, none are going to be perfect but each of them is capable of offering us something of value.

In the Garden of Gethsemane, Jesus chose three of his friends to share in his final grief. They weren't expected to say or do anything. He just wanted them there—"remain here and keep awake." One of the values of friends is simply that they are there; we don't necessarily need conversations or contact to know that they're thinking of us and would be there for us if we needed them.

Sometimes though, we need more than that. We need practical help or advice and we decide that one or more of our friends could provide it. It may have taken a struggle to get to that point. In the process we've put aside all sorts of reasons for not asking for help. Probably we've also assessed the risks. One is that they'll say no. There'll be some awkwardness about this, both at the time and for a while into the future. But better they do that than say yes when they are not really willing to offer the requested support. Perhaps they once said: "If I can do anything to help don't hesitate to ask," but didn't mean it and didn't seriously expect you to think that they did.

Another risk is that though they really do want to help and try their best to do so, they don't get it right. Their spirit is willing but their flesh is weak. This was the situation that confronted Jesus in Gethsemane. All he asked of his three followers was to keep alert but they couldn't even manage that. Their failure must simply have compounded his sense of loneliness and isolation.

A feeling of being let down is always a possibility, particularly when we try to talk through our situation with someone. There's value and release when we can share what we're going through but if our attempt to describe what we're experiencing doesn't seem to be understood (and it's asking a lot of someone to empathize with us if they've never been through anything similar themselves), or they make a comment which gives away their inability really to appreciate how we're feeling, the whole process can leave us feeling more on our own than if we'd never tried to explain it in the first place.

Part of the problem is that people who may well be sympathetic don't necessarily know what to say that will be really helpful. The disciples had this problem. The passage says they didn't know what to say to Jesus. It's true also that people who want to help us often don't know how to do it. They may well be inhibited by not wanting to be intrusive. In situations like this, we may need to have the courage not just to ask for help but to be precise about what kind of help would be useful. We're often afraid to do that, for fear of being thought demanding, but it's often really helpful for the person offering.

So seeking help may not be easy but it can be extremely rewarding. Many caregivers continue to feel they're struggling along on their own but others describe with a sense of wonder the way, often quietly and unobtrusively, help arrives when it's needed. Not just from family and friends either. It sometimes comes from people we don't even know. The young man who fled naked stayed with Jesus longer than the others. He had done what Jesus wanted without even being asked and had watched with him. Perhaps as we work out how best to seek support from our friends and families, people we don't even know will be to us like angels sent from God.

That's how a different version of the story we're looking at describes the support Jesus experienced in Gethsemane. St Luke's account says that as he prayed, angels came and strengthened him. Jesus had gone there to pray—his praying was not full of words but it came out of his deep grief and fear. He didn't get the release from what lay ahead that he pleaded for. But, as the angels symbolize God gave him the support he needed. However it comes, support is what caregivers need in what can be otherwise a lonely task.

Some possibilities for discussion
- Share good tips about how to ask for help.
- How do you deal with offers that aren't quite what you need?
- Do you share your situation with God? Jesus prayed to be released from the situation he was in. What do you pray for? Does it change anything?

Learning

Brother Lawrence was a lay brother in a Carmelite Monastery during the seventeenth century. After his death, some of his conversations and letters were gathered into a book entitled *The Practice of the Presence of God.*

He suggests that religion has been made too complicated. It's really very simple—if we do everything, including the most insignificant and mundane daily tasks, out of love for God, we shall eventually begin to experience his presence. Simple, he says, but not easy. It requires discipline, constantly recalling God's presence to mind when it seems to be wandering away.

Today's theme has been a reminder to seek human support in our caregiving. Brother Lawrence's writing reminds us that God is also there for us in caregiving's joys and rewards and also in its most humdrum and tedious moments. Brother Lawrence suggests that God's presence is with us always; what we need to do is become aware of it.

Some possibilities for discussion

- There are different ways of reminding ourselves of God's presence during a busy day—strategic placing of an appropriate picture, placing an object with religious associations in your pocket or handbag, listening to religious music or radio. What ways have you found helpful? How could you help yourself to practice the presence of God?
- Is it appropriate to include the person you care for in this process? If so, how might you do that?

Preparing for the next session

In the next session, we shall be talking about a story by Margery Williams called *The Velveteen Rabbit.* You can read the story in its entirety or find summaries of it if you google "Velveteen Rabbit" or by following the links on www.caring-together.com.

Prayers

Leader   Be strong and courageous; do not be frightened or dismayed, for the Lord your God is with you wherever you go. *(Joshua 1:9)*

Now is the time for anyone in the group to mention anything going on in their lives that they are finding difficult. When there has been time for everyone who wishes to speak, a silence follows, during which each quietly prays for the members of the group who have just spoken. Anyone who wishes to say a prayer out loud can also do so.

> Generous God,
> as we pray for each other, you meet us in our need.
> Grant us the resources we need for our caregiving
> and surround us with your love.
> **Amen.**
>
> Jesus said: "Peace I leave with you; my peace I give to you. I do not give to you as the world gives. Do not let your hearts be troubled, and do not let them be afraid." *(John 14:27)*

Now go around the group in turn and each person mention the name of someone they are caring for. Follow each mention by a long enough silence for that person to be prayed for silently by the group before the next person speaks. Then all pray together:

Loving God,
you promise to sustain all whose lives are hard.
Grant those for whom we care
your strength and your peace.
Amen.

May God bless us all till we meet again.
Amen.

To take away

And the one throwing the lifebelt,
Even he needs help at times,
Stranded on the beach,
Terrified of the waves.

"Waves," Brian Patten

Session 9

Growing through Pain

In this session, we will look at whether it's possible to use the suffering and struggle we experience as a resource for our own personal growth.

Opening reflection
Listen to "The Skye boat song" (available to download from www.kevinmayhew.com/caring-together-download.html or from www.caring-together.com).

The song recalls the escape of Bonnie Prince Charlie after his defeat at the Battle of Culloden in 1746 and his followers' belief that there was hope even in defeat.

A prayer to say together
Generous God,
you knew what it was like to feel defeated by suffering
but out of it you emerged stronger than before.
Help us to learn from every situation that confronts us.
May the winds and waves that others feel may swamp us
be for us the pathway to new discoveries.
Carry us forward,
through every experience that threatens defeat,
into a new hope for the future.
In the name of your Son, Jesus.
Amen.

Gathering
Each person should take about a minute to give their name and describe someone suffering in some way who they admire.

Exploring

Of Mary Craig's four sons, Paul suffered from gargoylism and Nicky from mongolism. In her book, *Blessings*, she describes how she enabled the experience to become a creative one.

> When I finally stopped feeling sorry for myself, I found myself beginning to think deeply about the whole problem of grief and suffering in our lives. More and more I was convinced that, though suffering was itself negative, it could very easily destroy. On the other hand it could be used positively, for growth. It was, in fact, the only means of emotional growth, the route from winter to spring. "Your pain," wrote Kahlil Gibran, in "The Prophet," "is the breaking of the shell that encloses your understanding. Even as the stone of the fruit must break, that its heart may stand in the sun, so must you know pain." That seemed to me to reach the heart of the matter. I knew that, in my own case, however hard I had been trying to come to terms with the tragedy, I had in effect been shutting out the pain, trying to deaden my awareness of it, allowing a rock-hard shell to form and insulate me from it . . . Building up the shell *was* an answer, but in the end it was a rotten answer; and until that shell could be smashed, there was no hope of personal growth.
>
> It was all a question now of learning to take this new pain into myself so that it could become creative. To do that, I should have to face the facts head on, hiding nothing, neither exaggerating nor playing down. To see my situation exactly as it was, to go forward from there, that was the secret.
>
> Inevitably that could only be a beginning, but it was a good one . . . the land ahead is unknown, and the roads are all uncharted. "Here be dragons" a-plenty, but the

worst enemy, that composite of self-delusion and self-pity, has been identified, and at least some of its power to destroy has gone.

Some possibilities for discussion
- Is there anything in this account that rings a bell for you?
- In what ways do you think suffering can "very easily destroy"?
- "Building up the shell *was* an answer, but in the end it was a rotten answer." Can protecting yourself from pain sometimes be appropriate? Or is it always a "rotten answer"?
- Mary Craig suggests that letting herself really feel the pain was the pathway to a new beginning. Is this true for you?

Reflecting

Making space for reflection:

Someone reads from Matthew 4:1-11

> Then Jesus was led up by the Spirit into the wilderness to be tempted by the devil. He fasted for forty days and forty nights, and afterwards he was famished. The tempter came and said to him, "If you are the Son of God, command these stones to become loaves of bread." But he answered, "It is written, 'One does not live by bread alone, but by every word that comes from the mouth of God.'"
>
> Then the devil took him to the holy city and placed him on the pinnacle of the temple, saying to him, "If you are the Son of God, throw yourself down; for it is written, 'He will command his angels concerning you,' and 'On their hands, they will bear you up, so that you will not dash your foot against a stone.'" Jesus said to him, "Again it is written, 'Do not put the Lord your God to the test.'"
>
> Again, the devil took him to a very high mountain and showed him all the kingdoms of the world and their splendour; and he said to him, "All these I will give you,

if you will fall down and worship me." Jesus said to him, "Away with you, Satan! For it is written: 'Worship the Lord your God, and serve only him.'" Then the devil left him, and suddenly angels came and waited on him.

Comments

(If you would like to hear the author reading these himself please refer to www.caring-together.com)

One value of a group like this is that it offers a chance to step back for a while from the routine demands of our lives. Such stepping back helps puts things in perspective. I remember the broadcaster Frank Topping once saying that at times of stress, he would go for thirty seconds in his mind's eye to a lovely peaceful beach on the west coast of Scotland. When he came back mentally into the hurly burly of the studio, he was much more relaxed and effective. We could all benefit from learning techniques like that! If you try it, make sure you really go there —hear the sounds, smell the smells!

But there are times when longer periods of distancing can also help. They not only defuse any tension, they also provide an opportunity to reflect on what is going on under the surface of our lives and what we can learn from what we're experiencing. When Jesus took time out in the wilderness, he hoped his reflections on his life so far would help him discover what God wanted him to do with the rest of it. He needed to work out what sort of caregiving he should be offering God's people.

Perhaps one temptation we experience as caregivers is to look for unhelpful short cuts and quick fixes. There's the deep longing of most of us that the person we care for suddenly recover—a longing that's no less powerful because it's unlikely or impossible; there's the more superficial day-to-day temptation to be a bit slapdash or hurried in our caregiving so that we can get on more quickly with something else; and in between there's a whole range of ways in which we're tempted to escape from the demands of our situation. The suggestion that Jesus might turn stones into bread not only offered a quick end to the hunger of fasting; if he'd been able regularly to do it, it would have been a quick way to people's hearts, a way to avoid more costly but more profound ways of revealing God's love of them. But Jesus rejected it—it wasn't God's way.

The second temptation Jesus faced was to prove himself. If he were to be saved from harm when he hurled himself from the pinnacle of the temple, there would be no doubt he was somebody very special. A much more effective and immediate way of establishing his credentials than the hard grind of daily loving. All of us want recognition, we want to be valued. As caregivers, we want the person we're looking after to appreciate us and one of the hardest kinds of caregiving is when the person concerned is not capable of expressing that kind of gratitude. And when they can but don't, it can hurt. Most of us also want to be recognized for what we're doing by others, family members, neighbors, fellow church member(s). It may be tempting to do or say something that will provoke that kind of recognition yet we know, as Jesus did, that the true motivation for our caregiving must be to love the one cared for, not gather accolades for ourselves.

In the third temptation Jesus was offered all the kingdoms of the world. But this would be at the cost of doing things Satan's way. "Worship the Lord your God and serve only him," Jesus tells Satan. "I want to do things God's way." "Doing things God's way" means something different for each person. But we need to be careful not to think it necessarily implies continuous self-sacrifice. As we saw in Session 2, God's will for us is that we care for ourselves as well as others.

After that, the devil left him. But the way Jesus dealt with his various temptations had helped him grow into an understanding of what his role should be. His standing back for a while gave him the chance to use the thoughts and feelings he was having to move him forward into a clearer awareness of himself. His desert experience made him a stronger person. We may have very different temptations from Jesus. Our reactions to the situation we're in are going to be different from anyone else's. But taking time to reflect on them can make us stronger.

It can be tempting not to bother. The process requires energy that may be in short supply. It requires being disciplined enough to find the time, also something we may not have much of. It may be painful as we break through the shells we've built into our psyches and discover feelings and motivations of which we may be far from proud. But the result of doing it will be to make us, as it made Jesus, stronger, more aware of ourselves and therefore of what we are able to offer others. We'll find the resources to enable us to avoid unhelpful short cuts in our caregiving, to manage without constant affirmation from others for what we're doing, and to be open to God in a way that means we do things his way. And we may well discover, as Jesus did, that one result of our courage in facing these issues is that "angels come and wait on us."

Some possibilities for discussion
- What kinds of temptations do those who care for others have to deal with?
- Jesus used his time in the wilderness to discover who he was meant to be. What is our caregiving teaching us about ourselves?
- Is it important to stand back occasionally and gather your feelings and thoughts? How can you make time for such reflection? What could you do in the coming days to find time for it?

Learning

Margery Williams' story *The Velveteen Rabbit* tells of a toy rabbit that becomes real as it loves and is loved by the Boy whose toy he is. The story emphasizes that this happens through, and because of, the rough and tumble of sharing the Boy's life. Here is a key section:

> "What is REAL?" asked the Rabbit one day, when they were lying side by side near the nursery fender, before Nana came to tidy the room. "Does it mean having things that buzz inside you and a stick-out handle?"
>
> "Real isn't how you are made," said the Skin Horse. "It's a thing that happens to you. When a child loves you for a long, long time, not just to play with, but REALLY loves you, then you become Real."
>
> "Does it hurt?" asked the Rabbit.
>
> "Sometimes," said the Skin Horse, for he was always truthful. "When you are Real you don't mind being hurt."
>
> "Does it happen all at once, like being wound up," he asked, "or bit by bit?"
>
> "It doesn't happen all at once," said the Skin Horse. "You become. It takes a long time. That's why it doesn't happen often to people who break easily, or have sharp edges, or who have to be carefully kept. Generally, by the time you are Real, most of your hair has been loved off, and your eyes drop out and you get loose in the joints and very shabby. But these things don't matter at all, because once you are Real you can't be ugly, except to people who don't understand."

Some possibilities for discussion

- How is the caregiving you are doing changing you?
- Do you feel you're able to be "real" with the person you're caring for? And with others?

Preparing for the next session

In the next session, we shall be exploring Martin Buber's I-Thou concept. Follow the links on www.caring-together.com or google "I-Thou."

Prayers

Leader Jesus said: "I came that they may have life, and may have it abundantly." *(John 10:10)*

Now is the time for anyone in the group to mention anything going on in their lives that they are finding difficult. When there has been time for everyone who wishes to speak, a silence follows, during which each quietly prays for the members of the group who have just spoken. Anyone who wishes to say a prayer out loud can also do so.

> Generous God,
> as we pray for each other, you meet us in our need.
> Grant us the resources we need for our caregiving
> and surround us with your love.
> **Amen.**
>
> The Lord is near to the broken-hearted, and saves the crushed in spirit. *(Psalm 34:18)*

Now go around the group in turn and each person mention the name of someone they are caring for. Follow each mention by a long enough silence for that person to be prayed for silently by the group before the next person speaks. Then all pray together:

> **Loving God,
> you promise to sustain all whose lives are hard.
> Grant those for whom we care
> your strength and your peace.**

Amen.

May God bless us all till we meet again.
Amen.

To take away

Help me in my search for reality. Be real, really yourself, really present, with me. And shine a torch on me that I may see myself as I truly am.

> *Jim Cotter, a writer and theologian who in May 1994 experienced a sudden breakdown, addressing his caregivers*

Session 10
The Struggle and the Joy

In this last session, we will look at some of the challenges and some of the rewards of our caregiving.

Opening reflection

Listen to "You'll never walk alone" (available to download from www.kevinmayhew.com/caring-together-download.html or from www.caring-together.com).

A prayer to say together
Reliable God,
thank you for those who accompany us
in the journey of our lives,
for their support during the stormy times.
Your care for us is expressed through them.
But sometimes we still feel very alone.
Thank you for the confidence we get
from knowing that, however strong the wind and rain,
you will never leave us.
Through your Son, Jesus.
Amen.

Gathering

Each person should take a minute to give their name and say something about themselves the rest of the group may not yet have discovered.

Exploring

In the last of the extracts from books and articles written by caregivers, here's a poem written anonymously for an anthology compiled by the Manchester Carers Centre from material written during a creative writing workshop for caregivers.

"You and Me"
Occasionally,
not very often,
I get encouragement
and recognition
and that makes me feel good
and keeps me going.

More often
I feel sad,
frustrated,
taken for granted,
angry
at no life
to call my own.

And then
you smile
and I look at you.
It's hard to say
it's not worth it
because you are.
Even if it means
I merely exist.

Some possibilities for discussion
- Is there anything in this poem that rings a bell for you?
- Do you ever feel your caregiving is taken for granted? Where do you look for, or find, encouragement when that happens?

- The poet says that they "merely" exist, implying perhaps that they are missing out on a full experience of living. Is that true of your experience of caregiving?
- This poem emerged from a group of caregivers that met to share their experiences and express them creatively. In what ways has this group been valuable for you?

Reflecting

Looking and loving:

Someone reads from Luke 10:38-42

> Now as [Jesus and his disciples] went on their way, he entered a certain village where a woman named Martha welcomed him into her home. She had a sister named Mary, who sat at the Lord's feet and listened to what he was saying. But Martha was distracted by her many tasks; so she came to him and asked, "Lord, do you not care that my sister has left me to do all the work by myself? Tell her then to help me!" But the Lord answered her, "Martha, Martha, you are worried and distracted by many things; there is need of only one thing. Mary has chosen the better part, which will not be taken away from her."

Comments

(If you would like to hear the author reading these himself please refer to www.caring-together.com)

It's not difficult to leap to Martha's defense. Someone has to prepare the meals, do the housework, keep the show on the road. We can't all just drop everything because something we'd prefer to be doing comes along. And her resentment may ring a bell for you too. There she is, struggling away, and not a finger is being lifted to help her. We might want to suggest to Martha that if she'd been on this course, learned to take care of herself as well as others, searched out appropriate support, found ways of turning her frustration into creative energy, she'd have remained much calmer! But even we who have had the chance to discuss all that, still occasionally identify with her feeling of being taken for granted and dumped on.

The anonymous writer of the poem you've just been discussing certainly felt that. But then the person they are caring for smiles and suddenly it's all worth it. Of course there might have been gratitude and appreciation in the smile. That would certainly dissipate the sense of being taken for granted. But it doesn't read as though that's what's contributed to the change of attitude. It is more that the author really sees the person they are caring for and their unique, extraordinary humanity, a beauty which is being enhanced by the relationship between them, and then the struggle becomes a joy.

We don't know the situation of the person the writer is caring for. It may be that they are not physically capable of much at all. It may not be possible to have any verbal communication with them, as is the case for some people with Alzheimer's or autism for example. But that makes no difference to the sense the writer has of the wonder of their existence and the beauty of who they are. In that profound moment of really seeing, what is being experienced is a profound respect, a dignified acceptance, and an enchanted delight.

Martin Buber, whose ideas we'll be looking at later, suggested that we look for this kind of moment of insight in all our relationships. And he went on to say that in such interactions between human beings, there is insight into the true nature of our relationship with God. That too is characterized by respect, acceptance, and delight in each other. But such relationships don't just bring insight into our relationship with God, they are part of it. As we look at another with warmth, appreciation, and reverence because of who they are, we are looking at something of God. Mother Teresa tells how outside the convent in Calcutta, the feeble cries coming from a trash can turned out to be those of a very frail, elderly, sick old man. "No one is trash," she said and went on to speak not only of the humanity of each person but of the divine that is also in them. Every human being is made in God's likeness. As George Fox, founder of the Quakers, put it, "Walk cheerfully over the earth answering that of God in everyone."

I think that's what we're doing in our caregiving. Each of the people we care for is God's gift to us. In them there is something of God. In our cherishing of them, we are answering that of God that is in them. And strangely, the more we treasure their individuality, their particularity, the more we open ourselves to a wider, more general awareness of God's presence in everything. When we sit at the feet of the ones we care for as Mary sat at the feet of Jesus, as we look at the ones we care for with the same expectancy and delight as she looked at Jesus, we find Jesus looking back at us.

Martha's problem may well have been that she had lost sight of why she was doing all that work. Like some of us, she may have felt she had no choice; like us, she may have felt wearied by the relentless organizing and physical hard work involved in caring for Jesus; she may justifiably have felt taken advantage of. But if she had taken a moment to stop as Jesus seems to be suggesting and do the one thing needed; if she'd done what Mary was doing and really, really, for however short a time, looked at the one she was rushing about caring for, her whole feeling about it might have been quite different.

I hope you have found these sessions valuable. Thank you for using this material. I hope it has encouraged you. I hope it will give you renewed energy for the task, in Fox's words, of walking cheerfully, answering that of God in the people you care for.

Some possibilities for discussion

- Are there times when busyness gets on top of you? What are the symptoms? And the cure?
- In the poem we looked at, it's a smile that helps the caregiver really to look at the one they're caring for. Share moments when you've been able to really see the one you care for. How can you make it happen more often?
- What difference does it make to think of the person you care for as "made in the likeness of God"?

Learning

The philosopher Martin Buber distinguishes between two types of human relationship. The first is functional—for example, someone we interact with at work or as we shop or travel, usually with the sole purpose of achieving a task. This kind of relationship he describes as I-It. The other kind are I-Thou relationships. In these, the relationship with the other is more personal; the meeting of the two people is at a much deeper level, person to person. Whereas in an I-It relationship the other person may be seen simply as an object that is useful in achieving a particular purpose, in an I-Thou relationship, there may be no particular purpose for the relationship but through it each is affirmed and valued.

Buber is not criticising I-It relationships—they are a necessary part of life—nor is the character of a relationship fixed. An I-It relationship with the person checking out our groceries, for example, can become an I-Thou one if we have a conversation with them; conversely, if we start taking a friendship for granted, riding roughshod over a friend's wishes, or using them to meet our needs without taking theirs seriously, an I-Thou relationship can become an I-It one.

The distinction is particularly important to Buber because he believes our relationship with God is an I-Thou relationship. It's not there to achieve any particular function, either for God or us, except that in the meeting of two persons both are affirmed.

Some possibilities for discussion
- Do you find the distinction between I-Thou and I-It relationships helpful?
- When might a relationship between caregiver and cared for become an I-It relationship?
- What would be the hallmarks of an I-Thou relationship between caregiver and cared for?
- Is your relationship with the person you care for teaching you anything about God and your relationship with God?

The next step

Take these final moments of the group to share ideas about whether any kind of follow-up would be helpful. Would members of this group like to go on meeting? If so, in what way? Are there other ways members of the group can continue to support each other? Are there other members of your congregation(s) who might find the course helpful? How could this be organized for them?

Prayers

Leader Those who wait for the Lord shall renew their strength, they shall mount up with wings like eagles, they shall run and not be weary, they shall walk and not faint. *(Isaiah 40:31)*

Now is the time for anyone in the group to mention anything going on in their lives that they are finding difficult. When there has been time for everyone who wishes to speak, a silence follows, during which each quietly prays for the members of the group who have just spoken. Anyone who wishes to say a prayer out loud can also do so.

> Generous God,
> as we pray for each other, you meet us in our need.
> Grant us the resources we need for our caregiving
> and surround us with your love.
> **Amen.**
>
> To you O Lord, I lift up my soul. O my God, in you I trust. *(Psalm 25:1-2a)*

Now go around the group in turn and each person mention the name of someone they are caring for. Follow each mention by a long enough silence for that person to be prayed for silently by the group before the next person speaks. Then all pray together:

> **Loving God,
> you promise to sustain all whose lives are hard.
> Grant those for whom we care
> your strength and your peace.
> Amen.**
>
> **May God bless us all till we meet again.
> Amen.**

To take away

I sought my soul, but my soul I could not see,
I sought my God, but he eluded me,
I sought my brother, and I found all three.

*Theodore K. Lawless,
medical researcher and philanthropist*

Appendix 1

Confidentiality

The value of a group like this will be greatly enhanced if members know they can speak openly without fear that what they say will be repeated outside the group. If they are to speak freely about the pressures they are under, they may need reassurance that no one will relay what they've said to the one they are caring for. The group must also decide whether it is appropriate to discuss outside the group, even with one of the group's members, something said in the group. On the whole this too is not helpful, though there may be times when to be too strict about this would prevent mutual support.

A common formula is that what arises in the group can be discussed in a general way but never to link any point to any particular person. In this way insights and issues of general relevance can be discussed without any individual's privacy being compromised. (If the leader is receiving support from someone in their leadership of the group, that relationship is exempt from these requirements.)

Some ground rules for discussions

The following sample list of ground rules is simply to aid your discussion—you may well have other points you want to raise but this is intended to help you get the ball rolling . . .

In this group:
- everyone's input is equally valued and their ideas, experiences, and feelings are respected.
- only one conversation happens at once (unless working in twos and threes).

- everyone is responsible for keeping the group focused; when conversation diverges from the set questions, this may lead to valuable discussion or to anecdotal chatting—everyone is equally responsible for avoiding the latter.
- it's appropriate to invite someone who hasn't spoken recently to say something but equally acceptable for them to decline. Verbal contributions are only one of the ways group members participate.
- body language and non-verbal responses are encouraging not disrespectful.
- judgmental comments are not acceptable; rather group members are invited to support each other and respect differences.
- everyone is responsible for making sure they don't take more or less of the group's time than is their proper share. Anyone who feels the group's time is not being appropriately shared should say so.
- when someone is speaking they are listened to without interruption.
- when what someone says is unclear, it's good to ask them to repeat it or explain it. For example, ask, "Can you say more about that?"
- everyone speaks from their own experience and avoids putting words into other people's mouths.
- people are not afraid to take risks. This can be anything from talking about personal issues to respectfully challenging another's opinion.
- we refrain from personal attacks.

Appendix 2
Notes on Structure

When the material for one session is spread over two meetings

If a second meeting is needed to complete the material in any of the sessions, I have provided a Bible reading below to replace the opening song. Do repeat the prayer from the "Opening reflection" section though. A different question for the "Gathering" section might also be useful so I have given suggestions for those too. Obviously your main discussion will be on the topics you didn't manage to cover the first time around. You might then want to repeat the same format for the prayers at the end of the session.

Session 1
Reading: 1 Corinthians 13:4-7.
Gathering: Each person gives their name and tells the group something they found helpful in the first meeting.

Session 2
Reading: Matthew 6:28-33.
Gathering: Each person gives their name and tells the group about an interest or hobby they have.

Session 3
Reading: Psalm 51:1-2, 10-12.
Gathering: Each person gives their name and tells the group about their most embarrassing moment.

Session 4
Reading: Isaiah 40:28-31.
Gathering: Each person gives their name and tells the group about a time they felt cared for.

Session 5
Reading: Mark 10:46-52.
Gathering: Each person gives their name and tells the group about a book or film they've enjoyed.

Session 6
Reading: Job 38:4-12 and 42:1-3.
Gathering: Each person gives their name and tells the group about someone they've learned a lot from.

Session 7
Reading: Ephesians 4:25, 26 and 4:31–5:2.
Gathering: Each person gives their name and tells the group about a treasured possession.

Session 8
Reading: Romans 12:4-13.
Gathering: Each person gives their name and tells the group about something they need.

Session 9
Reading: Isaiah 43:1-3a.
Gathering: Each person gives their name and tells the group about a favorite place.

Session 10
Reading: Joshua 1:5-7.
Gathering: Each person gives their name and tells the group something about themselves that they value.

Bibliography

Session 1
Ed. Geoffrey Duncan, *Wisdom is Calling*, Canterbury Press, Norwich, 1999.

Session 2
Sheila Cassidy, *Sharing the Darkness*, Darton Longman and Todd, 1988.

Session 3
Marianne Talbot, *Keeping Mum*, Hay House, 2011.
Elie Wiesel, *Souls on Fire*, quoted in Robert McAfee Brown, *Elie Wiesel-Messenger to all humanity*, University of Notre Dame Press, 1983.

Session 4
BBC Anthology, *The Light of Experience*, British Broadcasting Corporation, 1977.
Jack Kornfield, *After the Ecstasy, the Laundry*, Ebury Press, 2000.

Session 5
Ken Wilber, *Grace and Grit*, Gill and Macmillan, 2001.
Lawrence and Diana Osborn, *God's Diverse People*, Darton Longman and Todd, 1991 (for the description of the Myers-Briggs theory).
Anthony de Mello, *The Heart of the Enlightened*, Fount Paperbacks, 1989.

Session 6
Frances Young, *Face to Face*, T & T Clarke Ltd, 1990.

Frances Young, *Brokenness and Blessing*, Darton Longman and Todd, 2007.
Fynn, *Mister God this is Anna*, William Collins, 1974.

Session 7
Barbara Want, *Why not me? A story of love and loss*, Weidenfeld & Nicolson, 2010.
Sue Parker-Hall, *Anger, Rage and Relationship*, Routledge, 2009.
Joe Griffin and Ivan Tyrrell, *Release from Anger*, HG Publishing, 2008.
Stevie Smith, *The Collected Poems of Stevie Smith*, Penguin, 1985.

Session 8
Grace Sheppard, *Living with Dying*, Darton Longman and Todd, 2010.
Brother Lawrence, *The Practice of the Presence of God*, Wilder Publications, Limited, 2008 (also available for free legal download on the net: www.practicegodspresence.com/brotherlawrence/index.html).
Brian Patten, *Selected Poems*, Penguin, 2007.

Session 9
Mary Craig, *Blessings*, Hodder and Stoughton, 1979.
Margery Williams, *The Velveteen Rabbit*, Egmont Books Ltd, 2004 (also available for free legal download on the net: http://digital.library.upenn.edu/women/williams/rabbit/rabbit.html).
Jim Cotter, *Brainsquall*, Arthur James Ltd, 1997.

Session 10
Ed. Ged Neary, *Carers in the City*, Manchester Carers Centre, 2008.

www.ingramcontent.com/pod-product-compliance
Lightning Source LLC
Chambersburg PA
CBHW071214070526
44584CB00019B/3029